A WORLD
OF CHOCOLATE

INSPIRATIONAL RECIPES FROM THE WORLD'S BEST CHOCOLATIERS

NETWORK
BOOK PUBLISHING LTD

First Published in 2011 by
Network Book Publishing Ltd.

Network Book Publishing Ltd
28 Ballmoor, Celtic Court,
Buckingham, MK18 1RQ UK

www.networkpublishingltd.com

Printed by CT Printing Limited

ISBN 978-0-9567667-6-2

Printed in China

Publisher: Peter Marshall
Managing Editor: Shirley Marshall
Editor: Katy Morris
Recipe Editor: Sue Christelow
Editorial Assistant: Danielle May
Editorial Contributor: John Radford
Design Director: Philip Donnelly
Design: Jemma Pentney
Photography: Myburgh du Plessis, Ben Pollard
Ivan Frolov (Russian Photography)

FOREWORD

For chocolatiers there is always one event that is regularly marked in diaries and on calendars – the World Chocolate Masters. An event like no other, the competition is inspired by the world's favourite ingredient and gives chocolatiers, restaurant chefs and pâtissiers the opportunity to showcase the best of their culinary talents. A bi-annual event, the World Chocolate Masters is an initiative of Barry Callebaut. Barry Callebaut through its gourmet brands Callebaut, Cacao Barry and Carma, is the biggest global supplier of chocolate and related products for the chocolate professional.

After being fortunate enough to attend the event on many occasions I have regularly been awestruck by the fantastic desserts, mouth-watering pralines and the artistic showpieces that the contestants create in a brief amount of time. Despite the 'oohs' and 'ahhs' of the final pieces I would have to admit that my favourite part of the show is to watch the contestants in action particularly how their organisation and practise builds up to that ultimate point in the competition.

Months and months of preparation goes into this event and contestants do not take the privilege of contending lightly. The recipes that the contestants choose are carefully selected as the best that they can create. While the preparation that goes into every chocolate, every curl and every layer is outstanding, and the flavours so carefully tried and tested that classic combinations are reinvented, while new flavours work effortlessly in synchronisation ensuring that they become future classics.

There is a world of chocolate out there and only the World Chocolate Masters brings the highest standard of chocolate craftsmen together on a worldwide scale. For the contestants a chance to participate is everything and for the countries each and every one is proud to support their chosen contestant. It is this passion, support and love for fantastic chocolate that makes me delighted to be associated with this cookbook. As with Cacao Barry, Carma and Callebaut the contestants of the World Chocolate Masters donate their recipes to truly inspire a new generation of chocolatiers.

And with a selection of cakes, plated desserts and moulded and dipped praline recipes from across the globe, readers can truly enjoy a world of chocolate.

PETER MARSHALL

PUBLISHER

CONTENTS

THE HISTORY OF CHOCOLATE

THE WORD ITSELF IS BELIEVED TO HAVE BEEN DERIVED FROM XOCOLATL WHICH, IN THE NAHUATL LANGUAGE, MEANS 'BITTER WATER'. THE SPANISH CONQUISTADORES TRANSLITERATED THIS AS 'CHOCOLATE', AND THE ENGLISH SIMPLY ADOPTED THE WORD.

B y the time the Spaniards invaded what we now call central America, chocolate already had a long history. The cacao tree – Theobroma Cacao – grew wild about 20 degrees north and south of the equator, and the oldest archaeological evidence yet discovered indicates that the Olmec people had domesticated the tree and were making a drink from its pods as early as 1400BC, and by 1100BC it was well known to most of the peoples of central America, achieving its greatest prominence among the Aztecs and the Mayas around 400-500AD, who prized it as an expensive luxury, using it in votive rituals in honour of the plumed-serpent god Quetzalcoatl.

The beverage they made, however, bore not the slightest resemblance to the chocolate we know today. They would typically roast and grind up the beans and mix in chilli and other spices such as vanilla and achiote. On Columbus's fourth voyage in 1502, he arrived at the island of Guanaja, off the coast of what is now Honduras, and found merchant-traders with large canoes loaded with cargo, including xocolatl. Unfortunately he found it quite undrinkable and did no further research.

Opposite page: Ancient Drawing
Left to Right: Cocoa pod, Mayan culture, 500 AD, Chocolate mug with plate, 1710-1713 AD, Goblet for ceremonies, Mayan culture, 300-900 AD

Sixteen years later, in 1518, another Spanish explorer, Hernán Cortés, who was already resident in Cuba, led an army to conquer what is now central Mexico, and rediscovered the native drink, and also that it was so highly prized that the beans were used as currency: according to written records at the time an avocado could cost three beans, and a turkey 100 beans. In fact, rather than the drink itself, and cacao beans – nicknamed 'the gold of the New World' – were shipped back to Spain to be planted in the south of the country and in the north African colonies.

The native style still proved too bitter for the European taste and, as with so many drinks which have come down to us today, it was the monks who first added sugar to the bean paste and turned it into a sensation much enjoyed by the rich and royalty: it was still fabulously expensive. Within 100 years, however, the African plantations had made it much more affordable, and chocolate houses were established in major cities. The first in London was opened in 1657 by an anonymous Frenchman. The newspapers reported it thus: 'In Bishopsgate Street, in Queen's Head Alley, at a Frenchman's house, is an excellent West Indian drink called 'Chocolate' to be sold, where you may have it ready at any time and also unmade at reasonable rates.' Even then it was still very expensive, mainly the

A HAPPY FISHERMAN (ISLE OF MARKEN, HOLLAND)

Opposite page: Large pot ek chuah, Mayan culture, 300-600 AD
Top: Mould, 1920 AD
Bottom: Van Houten poster

preserve of the aristocracy, and a favourite of King Charles II. Such was its grip on fashionable London that in Sir John Vanbrugh's 1696 restoration comedy The Relapse, Lord Foppington, describing his daily routine to a lady upon whom he has designs, remarks: "If it be nasty weather, I take a turn in the chocolate-house where, as you walk, madam, you have the prettiest prospect in the world: you have looking-glasses all round you."

At this stage, chocolate was still served as a drink, and in 1689 Sir Hans Sloane (of Sloane Square and British Museum fame) first added milk to the mix while he was living in Jamaica. He called it 'Drinking Chocolate Milk' and it was the forerunner of what we might recognise today as drinking chocolate – indeed, he sold the formula to the Cadbury brothers in 1897.

The first non-liquid chocolate was made by J. S. Fry and sons in 1847. The company had been in the chocolate business since 1795, and Joseph Fry had adapted one of James Watt's steam engines to grind the beans, and he developed a process for binding the cocoa butter and cocoa solids together, with added sugar. The resulting paste could be solidified and became, effectively, the first chocolate bar.

The Victorian era was a time of major development for chocolate, which had become the favourite of Europe and,

thanks to mature plantations in Africa and industrialised machinery at home, very much more affordable. Innovation was everywhere: the cocoa press, which separated the cocoa solids from the cocoa butter, was invented by the Dutchman Conrad van Houten in 1828, Henri Nestlé had produced an evaporated milk powder which was added to chocolate by the Swiss chocolatier Daniel Peter in 1875, creating the first milk chocolate: he went on to team up with Henri to form the Nestlé company in 1879.

Modern methods have now made chocolate ubiquitous in every country of the world in styles that are about as far from the original Aztec/Mayan as it's possible to imagine, but its basic quality still relies on the beans of the cacao tree. Most production (and much of the best quality production) now comes from Africa, especially the Ivory Coast and Ghana. The process has been speeded up, refined and reinvented many times over the years, but the end result is the same: the raw material with which so many modern-day chocolatiers and pâtissiers ply their craft.

CALLEBAUT

In 1911, Eugène Callebaut – founder of the Callebaut company – became wildly enthused by something he experienced in Paris: chocolate. The seduction, mystery and indulgence of chocolate made him decide to start producing and perfecting his own. And what a start it was! Callebaut quickly partnered up with other Belgian chocolatiers, joining craftsmanship with creativity, and together they built the success and reputation of Belgian chocolate.

Belgian pastry makers and bakeries soon followed and after that, the whole world discovered the virtues of this noble product, known as the Finest Belgian Chocolate and a reputation Callebaut embodies wholeheartedly.

BUT WHAT IS IT THAT MAKES CALLEBAUT SO DIFFERENT AND UNIQUE?

THE HEART OF 'FINEST BELGIAN CHOCOLATE' LIES AT THE EQUATOR

One of the secrets of Callebaut's 'Finest Belgian Chocolate' can be found deep in the equatorial forests. The company is convinced that excellent chocolate can only be produced from first grade cocoa beans – whereas many chocolate makers today produce chocolate from purchased cocoa mass. To get access to the best crops, Callebaut is one of the very few

chocolate makers that still sources its own cocoa beans. Cocoa tracers travel through the cocoa-producing countries from Brazil to Malaysia to partner up with local co-operatives and farmers, and check the quality and potential of each harvest. Wherever possible, they buy directly from cocoa farmer co-operatives and in West Africa and Brazil, for instance, Callebaut works closely together with farmer co-operatives to set up new cultivation programmes. By improving cultivation methods developed together with bio-scientists, the company is dedicated to contributing to a brighter future for cocoa, cocoa farmers and their families – as well as maintaining the biodiversity in the delicate equatorial biotope.

PRECIOUS COCOA AROMAS FROM THE CORE OF THE COCOA BEAN

Cocoa is a difficult crop to cultivate but the most complex task starts after harvesting. Cocoa pods have to rest for approximately 24 hours after harvesting to fully ripen. Then they're opened to remove the beans with their pulp. A few days of fermentation under banana leaves makes the pulp drain away and awakens the full flavour potential that lies hidden in the core of each bean. Good fermentation is crucial to obtain chocolate to let taste and flavour shine through. Callebaut checks regularly on good fermentation practices and encourages and supports farmer co-operatives in order to achieve better results. The same goes for drying the beans after fermentation. Drying cocoa beans on wooden tables, so that they can bask in the sun's warming rays, gives the best results and leads to excellent quality chocolate.

THE MASTER ROASTER KNOWS EXACTLY WHEN THE FINEST AROMAS WILL BE UNLEASHED

When the cocoa beans arrive at the Callebaut warehouses in Europe, after weeks of shipping from Africa, South America or Asia, they are stored under the strictest of conditions. Once again, the cocoa beans undergo critical quality checks before they are blended. Beans from different origins are meticulously mixed to obtain the balanced blend that reveals the consistent flavours you know from Callebaut's 811, 823 and W2 – the stars of Belgian chocolate. The blend is composed in such a way that it will create a perfect balance between sweetness, bitterness, fruitiness, creaminess etc. once the chocolate is finished. It is exactly that well-balanced taste that lies at the root of Callebaut's success. Many professionals love working with these fine Belgian chocolates because they can easily customise it to their taste.

But it takes much more for the chocolate to reach its final form, in fact, the next step

is where the magic really starts. Backed by decennia of expertise, Callebaut's master roaster roasts the blend of cocoa beans to perfection: deep enough to bring out that overwhelming taste that is so typical for every Callebaut chocolate, yet mild enough to preserve even the most delicate flavours and top notes that add refinement. What's more, Callebaut is the only chocolate maker that roasts the cocoa beans in their shells – again to protect the more delicate notes in the cocoa. The roasted beans are then extremely finely ground into liquid cocoa mass. This cocoa mass which is completely prepared in-house is unique and really forms the heart and soul of Callebaut chocolate.

FINE, FINER, CALLEBAUT

The cocoa mass is then mixed with sugar and fine grade milk powder for milk chocolate couverture, transforming it into a dough. Callebaut refines this dough until every tiny little particle is smaller than the distance between human taste buds and impossible to detect separately in the mouth. This unique Callebaut feature guarantees the incredible homogenous and refined feel of the chocolate and its overwhelming taste in the mouth. During the hours of conching, all minuscule particles in the chocolate dough are enveloped with a thin layer of cocoa butter. This guarantees that when

chocolate melts in the mouth, the flavours will be released all at once – revealing the overwhelming Callebaut taste that goes from bittersweet to roasted fruitiness. Adding a dash of natural vanilla flavouring and the right amount of cocoa butter is the finishing touch. It's at this final moment – when all ingredients become one and melt together – that the chocolate merits its stamp of quality and authenticity as Callebaut 'Finest Belgian Chocolate'. It is now ready to be moulded in the big 5kg blocks or deposited as Callets™. It is exactly in this form – blocks or Callets™ – that Callebaut chocolate is so well-known to the thousands of artisan chocolatiers, pastry chefs and chefs that prefer the 'Finest Belgian Chocolate' above any other chocolate.

INNOVATING, BECAUSE THE FUTURE STARTS NOW

Besides its balanced taste and its unique fineness, there is more to this chocolate in order to make it unmistakably Callebaut. From the very beginning, Callebaut took on the role of innovator and from as early as 1925, the family investigated in ways to store and transport the chocolate in liquid form from the factory in Wieze – in the heart of Belgium – right to the customer's doorstep. It was quite a revolutionary feat for the time, and one of the first innovations of many.

When Callebaut's Callets™ saw the light of day in 1988, they sparked a true revolution in the chocolate world. By producing its chocolate in these small drops, Callebaut

instantly made its chocolates much easier to dose, melt and temper. That spirit of innovation continues today, with new chocolate recipes — such as Powerful 80%, a power bomb of a chocolate, and Velvet, a velvety white chocolate with just the right dash of sweetness. The new range of Fairtrade chocolates 811, 823, W2 and 70-30-38 now enable every professional to switch to Fairtrade without having to make even the slightest change to their recipes.

SOLID AS A BLOCK

Even today, after a century of chocolate craftsmanship, Callebaut keeps a keen eye on the typical, consistent taste and quality that make its chocolate couvertures unique. That's because they know how important that is for you and your success. Callebaut's customers from generation to generation and from father to son have experienced that the taste, the workability and the quality of Callebaut couvertures never changes so there is no need to add cocoa butter or cocoa liquor. Callebaut is dedicated to consistency — for today and tomorrow.

This year, Callebaut celebrates 100 years of the 'Finest Belgian Chocolate' and invites everybody who has played a part in its success — from cocoa farmers to Callebaut staff and you, its customers — to join the celebrations at **www.callebaut100years.com**

YOUR CRAFTSMANSHIP, CALLEBAUT'S PASSION

In the spirit of mutual inspiration, Callebaut enables its customers and staff to learn more about chocolate in its 13 Chocolate Academies. There they can follow practical and theoretical courses given by experienced technical advisors. The broad programme includes courses for beginning as well as more experienced professionals across all disciplines.

Course topics follow the latest trends and anticipate future ones, and the general course 'Starting with Chocolate' is the Chocolate Academy's bestseller and attracts professionals from around the world. It's the ideal basic course for every chef or professional wanting to understand the basic principles of chocolate processing: pre-crystallisation, hollow figures, pralines and more.

The courses mainly consist of practical assignments, which the students need to complete under the supervision of the technical advisors. These advisors are specialists in their profession and know the details behind Callebaut product. They test, contribute to the development of novelties, share advice about processing our products and give demonstrations all over the world. In their courses, they pass on as much knowledge as possible to professionals like you.

Also Callebaut's Chocolate Ambassadors pass on their chocolate know-how and techniques to other craftsmen. They form a vibrant network of leading, independent chocolate experts who work with Callebaut products and know them intimately. They represent Callebaut in the different markets, help the company test new products, and keep it informed about coming trends and changes in the markets. And so the two-way process continues, in a never-ending story of chocolate.

WHAT'S IN THE CALLEBAUT RANGE?

Finest Belgian Chocolate
Chocolates with a classic, balanced taste, in Callets™ or 5kg blocks.

Finest Selection
Chocolate with distinctive power and concentration from special cocoa blends.

Origine
Chocolate with unique flavours and aromas from rare cocoa crops.

Fairtrade
Chocolate with a heart for cocoa farmers.

Organic
Naturally good chocolate!

Chocolate with no added sugar
All the sweetness without the sugar.

Coloured & flavoured Callets™
Surprise with colour and flavour in your creations.

Chocolate for fountains
With added cocoa butter for the perfect liquidity.

Chocolate Mousse Powder
Tastes like homemade, ready in minutes.

Bake stable chocolates and pastes
Perfect for bakery and pastry products.

Coatings
The taste of chocolate without the need of pre-crystallising.

Icing & Decor Paste
Ready for your creativity.

Glazings
The brilliance of perfection, the true taste of chocolate.

Toppings & Sauces
The perfect complement to your creations.

Nut pastes
To add a naturally nutty twist.

Fillings
Exciting tastes and textures, ready to use.

Decorations & crunchy textures
The perfect finishing touch.

Semi-finished ingredients
For extra taste and colour.

Mycryo®
100% Cocoa butter in powder form.

Pure Sensation
Ready-to-use mix for the most delicious chocolate ice cream.

Find out more at www.callebaut.com

CACAO BARRY

PASSION AND CREATIVITY SINCE 1842

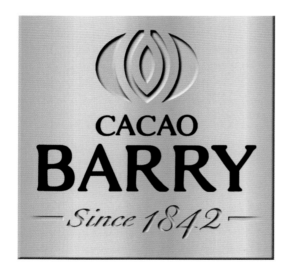

In 1842, starting out from the trade of tea and coffee, Charles Barry, a true innovator with a passion for chocolate, decided to go to Africa and seek out a selection of cocoa beans that would enable him to create his very first 'connoisseur's chocolate'. Named after Charles Barry, Cacao Barry continued to produce high quality chocolate and in 1963 Cacao Barry created chocolate baking sticks, and simultaneously the so famous pains au chocolat.

Innovative in terms of products, Cacao Barry was also the first brand to introduce personalised assistance and support to professionals in 1973. This passion for excellence can be seen today in Cacao Barry's premium couverture-chocolate recipes, which were developed by our own team of award-winning chefs.

Cacao Barry — where know-how and passion meet the enthusiasm of creative craftsmen demanding nothing but the best. By its passion for chocolate and intimate partnership, Cacao Barry enhances the creativity of all that use these fantastic products.

A FRENCH HERITAGE

Cacao Barry is recognised as a successful leader of confectionery in France and worldwide. Synonymous with famous French gastronomic heritage with a strong pastry expertise, the company works intimately with cocoa producers on their plantations in order to ensure the best quality harvest. This has a direct impact on the overall quality of beans used and allows Cacao Barry to select only the best and most appropriate beans for any specific chocolate recipe. More importantly, every single Cacao Barry product is made with 100 per cent pure cocoa butter and natural vanilla to ensure the highest quality level.

Chocolat à la Française is at the heart of our trade and expertise, but also at the heart of our customer's trade and expertise. It is the expertise of chocolate metamorphosis from a simple ingredient to finished artwork, the exceptional French tradition of pastry and couverture, the mystical alchemy which bonds chocolate passionate craftsmen, the heritage we want to pass on to future talents, supporting and inspiring people from school to academy, from new talents to icons.

A UNIQUE RANGE FOR UNIQUE PROFESSIONALS

Cacao Barry's passion for chocolate runs deep. The company is not content with simply producing and offering the finest premium chocolate in the world, instead it constantly strives to develop its product range and services in partnership with its customers.

Producing and marketing the finest-grade chocolate in the world, Cacao Barry has a wide product range that's a top favourite among leading chocolate professionals. A reliable quality of taste is the mark of high level chocolate, Cacao Barry controls each step from the selection of beans to the production of our exclusive chocolate recipes, including the production of our own cocoa butter. All our recipes guarantee a perfect consistency in taste as well as in technical features. This is the reason why each chocolate couverture from Cacao Barry is unique and so special. Using Cacao Barry products will provide you with the satisfaction of sustained quality, which will delight you and your customers over and over again!

PLANTATION MILLESIME

The exclusive Millesime plantations from Cacao Barry are made from specially chosen beans. They propose specific tastes and subtle variations that result from each year's changes in climatic conditions.

The plantation couverture chocolates offer a new vintage each year. On the same production cycle as wine, Cacao Barry's plantation range goes even further than the traceability process required by offering the best quality cocoa beans to its customers.

Also, Cacao Barry ensures a consistency in the products' taste as the beans are chosen from one unique plantation. The artisanal plantations from where the beans are provided offer a unique product. Always concerned by their partnerships with craftsmen, Cacao Barry proposes different recipes to its partners to enhance their creativity.

THE ORIGINE COLLECTION

Since 1842, chocolate professionals everywhere have recognised Cacao Barry as the creator of the finest and most exceptional chocolate couvertures. Always in search of new and original chocolate tastes, Cacao Barry has discovered a range of amazing cocoa beans, intense and rich, at the very furthest corners of the tropical world. From this variety of beans comes the Origine range: unique chocolate couvertures produced using beans harvested exclusively from the country whose particular soil, climate and cocoa variety define each chocolate as unique.

The Origine collection consists of eight chocolate couvertures: six dark chocolate couvertures and two milk chocolate couvertures. These chocolates of exceptional quality guarantee the culinary professional a variety of rich tastes and aromas to further improve the characteristics of their final chocolate creations.

INNOVATIONS

Cacao Barry is driven by excellence from the cocoa bean to the finished product. We share our long-standing passion for chocolate every day at our Chocolate Academies and our Ambassadors' Club, where we work to provide the most exacting artisans with targeted solutions. At Cacao Barry, we keep the tradition of excellence alive by innovating and by constantly striving to improve our mastery of the most complex and subtle of all ingredients: chocolate.

Cacao Barry was the first brand to offer the convenient Pistoles™ form of chocolate to craftsmen. Observing chefs using valuable time to break the 2.5 kg chocolate blocks to melt them, Cacao Barry decided to invent the Pistoles™ so that craftsmen can now concentrate their valuable time on their creations.

Cacao Barry innovations also include Pailleté Feuilletine™, Moulds and Mycryo® cocoa butter, a deodorised cocoa butter in powder form which is completely neutral. Mycryo® can be used in desserts, but also to temper chocolate and to enhance the colour, taste and texture of savoury food with break-through innovation created in 2003. Thanks to these unique products that enhance the creativity, Cacao Barry allows professionals to differentiate themselves, and to make their unique and daring chocolate fantasies come true.

SERVICES

Creative and strategic training has been an important Cacao Barry strategy for many years. Cacao Barry offers practical and theoretical courses for chocolate craftsmen: pastry chefs, confectioners, bakers and restaurant chefs. During practical courses, participants apply and broaden their technical skills under the guidance of a technical advisor or chocolate ambassador, while sharing experience and knowledge with other professionals. The famous Chocolate Academy in Meulan, France attracts worldwide pilgrims seeking the most exclusive dessert creations.

With the Ambassador Club, Cacao Barry encourages collaboration between professionals; the objective of this club is to transfer its chocolate know-how and techniques to other craftsmen all over the world. Quality, creativity, knowledge of ingredients and process leadership are the main assets of the Ambassador Club, present in more than 20 countries throughout the world.

Cacao Barry organises an exciting and challenging competition for chocolate talent, from all over the world: the World Chocolate Masters. This competition offers creative chocolate artisans the possibility to showcase their skills to an expert jury and public. The challenge is to withstand the stress of limited time and equipment, and to develop a top-level product around a specific theme. This competition is open to all creative chocolate talents.

Always seeking the best way to interact with professionals, a complete website is online and enables you to obtain information on our product range and special events in the chocolate world. You can also watch online demonstrations and chocolate courses as well as develop some printable labels and posters for your store.

Cacao Barry's passion drives everyone to set up new ideas and develop innovations to make the work of craftsmen easier.

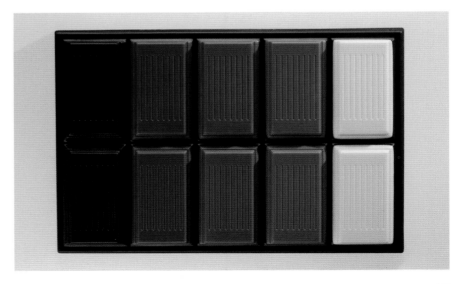

CARMA

A DELICIOUS EXPRESSION OF SWISS TRADITION

THE SWISS PARTNER FOR YOUR DESSERTS

When in 1931 Carl Maentler established Carma in Zurich, he wanted to launch high-quality ready-to-use products that would facilitate the work of pastry chefs. At that time he couldn't have imagined that some 80 years later his company would be one of the world's leading manufacturers of high-quality Swiss chocolate and ready-to-use dessert ingredients. Quickly establishing itself as the Swiss reference in gastronomy, hospitality, pastry and confectionery, Carma has always adhered to rigorous standards of excellence and consistent quality.

Backed by a clear commitment to its Swiss origin, Carma reflects the widely appreciated Swiss attributes – precision, reliability, accuracy and stability – in all its aspects. Switzerland has long had an outstanding reputation in the field of desserts, which is why many of the pastry chefs in quality restaurants around the world have Swiss roots. From the beginning, the company has also always been committed to innovation. With the introduction of a number of novelty products – from Massa Ticino, the white decoration paste, to compounds – Carma has changed the work of artisans, chefs and pastry chefs. That's how Carma has become the number one professional Swiss brand for making highly creative desserts.

A LONG HISTORY OF EXCELLENCE

Originally Carma only produced glazings – in Carl Maentler's apartment. Ten years after, the company moved to its Zurich-based production facilities and strawberry jam, decorations and later chocolate couvertures were added to the range. Carma's 30th anniversary in 1961 opened up new horizons and the Swiss gourmet and specialties brand started exporting to Asia and America. In the years that followed, Carma expanded its distribution to a broad customer base around the world.

When Carma joined the Barry Callebaut Group in 1999, Carma became the world manufacturer of Swiss chocolate for the group. It also began supporting the sales of the Barry Callebaut chocolate and cocoa products in Switzerland and it became clear instantly that both companies complemented each other very well.

CARMA SUPPORTS YOUR CREATIVITY

All Carma products are still developed in the Carl Maentler spirit. A pastry chef himself, he demanded that all his products were to be designed around a pâtissier's daily needs. Products are designed to make standard work processes in dessert production much more efficient. They are easy to work with and guarantee constant workability and performance and the Carma service offers support to

its customers to better use their products and develop creative applications. With the Swiss Chocolate Academy, for instance, Carma set up a place for dialogue, learning and knowledge exchange between its experts and its customers, to help them develop innovative approaches for the creation of delightful and exclusive desserts.

THE REFERENCE IN SWISS CHOCOLATE

The standard of Swiss chocolate is one of the highest in the world. Carma is at the forefront of this great chocolate-making tradition by keeping a high level of control on the quality of its chocolate, from the source to the finished product. The passion of Carma's experts, their dedication and their knowledge are the secrets to the brand's unique chocolate couvertures, which are celebrated for their unmatched premium quality, reliability and stability in all applications. In 2006, the distinguished Accademia Maestri Pasticceri Italiani dubbed Carma's 'Swiss Top' the best milk chocolate in the world. It received a record score for its unrivalled aroma, delectable auburn-brown tone, smoothness and consistent, lingering melt in the mouth.

Because the quality of the chocolate starts with the quality of the cocoa beans, the company sources its own beans from the equatorial regions in South America,

Africa and Asia. Only selected beans are pressed into cocoa mass and cocoa butter. By closely supervising the roasting of the cocoa beans and nibs, Carma guarantees a consistent quality of the unique Carma cocoa mass that is the base of all of its dark and milk chocolates.

Switzerland is most renowned for its silky smooth milk chocolate, that's why for its milk and white chocolates Carma only uses the highest quality Swiss milk that has a mild richness and adds to the smoothness of the chocolate. The velvety taste and texture of all Carma chocolates comes from the extra conching – a long, slow process that aerates the chocolate to remove any unwanted bitterness. Carma's conching technique also encourages a tiny bloom of cocoa butter to form around each particle of cocoa, making the chocolate homogenous and silky on the tongue. Finally, Carma uses natural vanilla – irreplaceable for its delicate flavour.

And it doesn't stop with just great taste. Outstanding workability is equally important. Therefore, Carma's unique cocoa butter provides slower crystallisation and longer workability. Carma's chocolates exhibit high temperature tolerance on tempering, which guarantees the best sheen, the finest glaze and the perfect snap.

THE SWISS PARTNER FOR YOUR DESSERTS

Carma's large range includes products that cover many pastry applications and that are perfectly aligned to offer complete dessert solutions, from chocolate couvertures to pastry bases, mousses, biscuits, glazings, icings, jams and gels.

Couvertures 'Origine Rare': each one produced with one single cocoa bean variety, reflecting unique aromas from outstanding crops.

Couvertures 'Swiss Top': made from carefully selected premium origin cocoa – the highest standard in Swiss chocolate.

Couvertures 'Swiss Line': made with excellent African blends and suitable for a wide range of applications.

Toppings & dessert sauces: with vanilla, chocolate or fruit – can be used hot or cold.

Mousses, flans, panna cotta: a full taste and light texture that melts in the mouth – ready in no time.

Pastry glazes: give an appetising gloss to your pastries.

Chocolate for interiors & specialties: unleash your creativity with these flakes, powders and modelling products.

Confectionery pastes, flavouring & gianduja: the perfect fillings for pralines and chocolate creations.

Sugar specialties & décor: versatile décor pastes, icing and decorations to turn any idea into reality.

Gels: the specialty of Carma – ideal for glazing fruit pastries.

Jams & fruit preparations: easy to apply, good baking performance and a delicious fruity taste.

Nut containing products: made with nothing but carefully chosen premium nuts.

For more information visit **www.carma.ch**

CARMA IN 5 WORDS

SWISS

Carma lets you experience the unique, authentic Swiss chocolate taste by using only the best ingredients including premium Swiss milk, and by adhering to the Swiss chocolate making tradition. Carma is proud of its Swiss heritage.

KNOW-HOW

Carma represents 80 years of experience in bakery, pastry and confectionery applications.

EXCELLENCE

Carma applies the highest standards on ingredients and production processes, offering you reliable solutions artisans can trust.

PROXIMITY

Carma's customers take centre stage in all its services. With its products and services, Carma supports artisans to create high-quality products.

AMBITION

Carma strives for innovation and continuously develops new products and solutions.

MAINTAINING QUALITY –
THROUGHOUT THE PROCESS

EVERYTHING BARRY-CALLEBAUT DOES DEPENDS ON THE SUPPLY OF THE RIGHT QUALITY COCOA, AND THAT DEPENDS ON THE QUALITY OF LIFE OF THE FARMERS AND THE SUSTAINABILITY OF THE PLANTATIONS.

The cacao tree is a delicate organism: it only grows in a narrow band of latitudes either side of the equator in Africa and central and south America, and some of these regions are amongst the poorest in the world. The main thrust of the company's policy, therefore, is to maintain the sustainability of the crop – harvesting sympathetically and in tune with nature – as well as helping the mainly small farmers who grow the crop to maximise their incomes and maintain and improve their quality of life.

In environmental terms the company is reducing its energy consumption and carbon emissions by such simple measures as turning the beans into cocoa liquor in their countries of origin (much cheaper than transporting the whole beans, and a provider of local jobs) and burning the waste products – the husks and shells of the pods – to provide power for the factories in Brazil, the Ivory Coast, Ghana and Cameroon. These methods cut down on transport and fuel consumption and, perhaps most importantly of all in these parts of the world where it can be a very precious commodity, water consumption.

At the farm level, Barry-Callebaut has several programmes to improve the efficiency and prosperity of the people who work on the land. These not only enhance the lives of the farmers but also, of course, ensure that yields are increased, which is good for local incomes, and the end-quality of the product continues to improve, which is good for the customer. One of these is the Quality Partner Programme, introduced in 2005. It starts with help in agricultural training: improving the fertility of the soil and the yields at harvest time, as well as help with pest control and disease management to maintain the health of the trees. The company offers interest-free loans to farmers who need to update their skills and equipment and, at a human level, there is also help with the provision of schools and health facilities for the farmers and their families in those areas where these are inadequate or even non-existent. By 2009 there were 47 co-operatives representing 42,000 individual farmers participating in the scheme.

Organic farming is another priority and the company made its first organic chocolate in 1996. In 2001 the Organic Cocoa Programme was launched in the state of Bahia in Brazil after an attack of a fungal disease which destroys the crop. Barry-Callebaut helped the local farmers first to eradicate the disease and then to convert their plantations to organic methods. They received certification in 2004 and by 2009 more than 4,000 hectares were in production, managed by 62 farmers.

Another investment was in 2008, when the company bought 49 per cent of the

Biolands project in Tanzania, having bought most of their production for several years previously. Biolands is one of the largest organic cocoa producing co-operatives in the world, and operates a system by which farmers are paid on delivery of the beans, with a follow-up payment at the end of the harvesting period. As well as cocoa beans, the project has supplied more than half a million seedlings for the plantation of new cacao trees in Africa. The co-operative also produces coffee, paprika, sesame and other tropical crops, all of which are paid for and sold under Fairtrade terms.

The commitment to children is part of the family-related programmes. Traditionally the children of farming families have helped out at harvest time (which is twice a year at these latitudes), especially in the poorest regions, and sometimes this has been viewed as exploitation. Barry-Callebaut does not own any farms or plantations, but buys cocoa beans from co-operatives and other farmers' organisations for processing locally. The company is, however, a member of the International Cocoa Initiative, which has strict guidelines on matters such as child labour, and has been involved with training farmers from more than 47 co-operatives to recognise the issues within their own communities. In the Ivory Coast, for example, the company funded

the establishment of a secondary school which opened in 2009 for 300 pupils. As well as normal educational subjects for the children, the curriculum majors on such important aspects as adult literacy, agricultural training and extra-curricular activities. Barry-Callebaut strongly and vigorously condemns any practices which exploit children and works with local authorities and communities to eradicate them, believing that the best way to help communities is education and a fair and decent price for their produce.

The final piece of the corporate responsibility is, of course, food safety.

This involves certification to international quality-assurance standards, product traceability, allergen management and, at the point of delivery, an absolute guarantee of quality and authenticity: there are chocolate products which are certified as kosher and halal, retail standards verified by the British Retail Consortium and International Food Standard and, of course, Barry-Callebaut is accredited to Fairtrade and the Rainforest Alliance as well as UTZ 'Good Inside', to provide total confidence for the customer. The word 'utz', incidentally, means 'good' in the Mayan language which is, of course, where the whole chocolate business began.

BARRY CALLEBAUT'S WORLD-WIDE CHOCOLATE EDUCATIONAL PROGRAMME

BARRY CALLEBAUT IS THE LARGEST SUPPLIER OF HIGH QUALITY CHOCOLATE TO THE WORLDWIDE ARTISAN CRAFT MARKET. BARRY CALLEBAUT'S RELATIONSHIP WITH PROFESSIONALS HAS BEEN BUILT UPON A GLOBAL DETERMINATION TO EDUCATE OF CHEFS, CONFECTIONERS, PATISSERIES AND BAKERS ON THE VERY BEST CHOCOLATE PRACTICES.

This educative approach is built upon a the foundation of 13 Chocolate Academies, each of which provides the heart of a comprehensive global strategy to provide chocolate education through the whole of a chocolate craftsman's career, from novice to chocolate master.

This training is directed to ensure that professionals anywhere in the world have easy access to utilise the creative and commercial opportunities offered by chocolate. The Barry Callebaut approach is to provide expert training as locally as possible, in native languages and modified to local requirements.

A worldwide Chocolate Academy website allows professionals to view courses and events around the world in nine languages and to book their requirements online.

The worldwide Academies network can train up to 500 professionals per week – practical training courses and demonstrations, theory and one-to-one practical courses. The Academies host more than around 350 courses each year in the 13 Academies and provide almost 1000 external training's per year in schools, hotels, customer kitchens, exhibitions and at special events.

For those unable to visit actual events, the skills of the Barry Callebaut academicians are made available to craftspeople throughout the world via a

range of around 50 films appearing on the Callebaut, Carma, Cacao Barry and Chocovic websites. These websites are full of useful information relating to all aspects of chocolate skills, techniques, tips and tricks.

Barry Callebaut has sought to support horeca, bakery, pâttiserie and confectionery schools throughout the world by the provision of an educational kit designed in nine languages which gives teachers a range of chocolate teaching aids including presentations, samples, detailed teaching notes, student activities and especially prepared films.

Barry Callebaut also leads an 'Association of the World's 30 Leading Chocolate Schools' which seeks to recommend ongoing improvements in the communication and teaching of chocolate skills. All Barry Callebaut teaching is targeted on artisans of all skill levels who share a common desire to improve their working skills in chocolate and learn about new trends, techniques and recipes.

Practical curriculum's include beginner, advanced and specialised courses on chocolate processing and a range of techniques and applications. Theory curriculum's include focused training on food labeling, marketing techniques, display concepts, innovative packaging and staff training directed to allow artisans to

better sell their offer to end consumers.

Training is conducted by a mix of Barry Callebaut's full time Technical Advisors and Chocolate Ambassadors with particular and high level specialisations.

Chocolate Ambassadors are an association of leading chocolate professionals selected for their quality, creativity, chocolate knowledge and process leadership who share Barry Callebaut's passion to communicate its love of chocolate and its pride in chocolate skills to the world.

Barry Callebaut's gourmet brands have taken a lead in organising a World Chocolate Masters Competition which through 20 national pre-selection competitions and a World Final seek to promote the very best in Chocolate craftsmanship. The competition seeks to celebrate the greatest chocolate artisans as a means of enthusing youngsters in the chocolate industry to perfect their own chocolate skills and strive themselves for the title of World Chocolate Master.

WHY IS THIS TRAINING SO GOOD?

Because Barry Callebaut understands cocoa and chocolate better than any other company. It is the only fully-integrated global chocolate manufacturer looking after all aspects of the process from bean to shelf.

Because Barry Callebaut is present in all countries throughout the world, its training is uniquely built upon an awareness of different chocolate cultures and customer expectations.

Because Barry Callebaut is the heart and engine of the chocolate industry pioneering innovative chocolates products and applications, its training reflects the latest product innovation and most modern commercial trends.

Because Barry Callebaut has integrated its internal Technical Advisors with leading professionals throughout the world to ensure its courses reflect the latest artisanal techniques and product design.

Because the Barry Callebaut Academies are integrated within a single chocolate network to help create a global chocolate culture, its training reflects the very best common practices around the world.

WHAT ARE THE ADDITIONAL FUNCTIONS OF THE CHOCOLATE ACADEMIES?

To provide a platform for the presentation of Barry Callebaut product solutions and services.

To concentrate chocolate knowledge in centres of excellence in order to facilitate partnerships with artisans.

To provide a forum for dialogue with

customers through seminars and customer focus groups.

To provide an institute to pioneer new chocolate products, applications techniques and recipes.

To provide an expertise where customer communication such as websites, leaflets, products and information can be designed to better relate to actual customer needs.

To provide an institution designed to spread a global chocolate spirit and culture through excellence.

WHO ARE THE CHOCOLATE AMBASSADORS WHO SUPPORT THE ACADEMY?

An association of leading chocolate professionals selected for their quality, creativity, chocolate knowledge and process leadership.

Recruited by invitation only.

A vibrant live network that unites more than 100 chefs, pastry chefs, master bakers and confectioners of international reputation.

All share a common mission to transfer chocolate know-how and techniques to other craftsmen all over the world.

All are expert practitioners of Callebaut, Carma or Cacao Barry brands.

All are charismatic and credible teachers of a full range of chocolate techniques.

WHAT IS THE WORLD CHOCOLATE MASTERS?

The worlds premium international culinary competition devoted solely to the creative use of chocolate in all its applications.

The only truly global culinary competition based on world wide national selection competitions as well as an international final.

Specifically designed to showcase the very best practice in contemporary chocolate.

Open to any of the world's most talented chocolate craftsmen and women – the winner becoming World Chocolate Master.

Designed to promote personality, audacity and ingenuity of the chocolate world support excellence and lead the pursuit of the highest standards of skill and creativity.

WHAT IS THE INTERNATIONAL SCHOOL ASSOCIATION?

A network of more 30 high level culinary schools from around the world defined as Chocolate Academy Associates.

Recruited by invitation only.

Selected for the quality of teaching, creativity of students, chocolate expertise and professional leadership in their countries.

A vibrant live network built on a shared vision to improve the communication and teaching of chocolate know-how and techniques to young craftsmen.

An association benefiting from the provision of intimate relations with Chocolate Academies, the exchange of staff and the provision of teaching tools.

Schools include the Joviat school in Spain, Westminster and Birmingham colleges in Great Britain, Lenôtre and Ferrandi in France, Bruges, Antwerp and Brussels in Belgium etc.

ACADEMY LOCATION

EUROPE

BELGIUM

Barry Callebaut Belgium. Alstersestraat 122, B-9280 Lebbeke Wieze, Belgium
Tel: +32 53 73 02 99, Fax: +32 53 78 05 40
Technical Advisors: Philippe Vancayseele, Alexandre Bourdeaux
Administrator: Sonja Van den Bossche

FRANCE

Barry Callebaut France, 5 Boulevard Michelet, Hardricourt, 78250 Meulan, France
Tel: + 33 (1) 30 22 86 22, Fax : + 33 (1) 30 22 87 57
Technical Advisors: Philippe Bertrand, Martin Diez
Administrator: Nadia Neveu

GREAT BRITAIN

Barry Callebaut UK, Wildmere Road, Industrial Estate, Banbury OX16 3UU, England
Tel: +44 1295 224 755, Fax: +44 1295 224 780
Technical Advisor: Beverley Dunkley
Administrator: Julie Buckland

POLAND

Barry Callebaut, Ul. Snowy Józefów 36, Lódz, 94-406 Poland
Tel: + 48 42 683 77 74, Fax: + 48 42 683 77 01
Technical Advisor: Marcin Pazdzior

SPAIN

Ctra. Nacional 152a, km 71,3
08503 Gurb
Tel: +34 938 893 419

SWITZERLAND

Barry Callebaut AG, Westpark, Pfingstweidstrasse 60, CH-8005 Zurich, Switzerland
Tel: +41 43 204 04 97, Fax: +41 43 204 05 09
Technical Advisors: François Stahl
Administrator: Daniele Pollice

THE NETHERLANDS

De Ambachten 35, 4881 XZ ZUNDERT
Tel: +31 76 597 8300, Fax: + 3176 597 6493
Technical Advisor: Ton Jongejan
Administrator: Joleen Becu

AMERICA

CANADA

Barry Calleabaut, 2950 Nelson Street, J2S 1Y7 St Hyacinthe
Tel: + 1-450-261-2131 / +1 450-774-9131, ext. 2432, Fax: +1 450 778 56 26
Technical Advisor: Derrick Tu Tan Pho
Coordinator: Denise Duhamel

USA

Barry Callebaut, 600 West Chicago Avenue, Suite 860, Chicago IL 60654
Tel: +312-496-7427 /ext. 7427, Fax:: +312 496 7399
Technical Advisors: Patrick Peeters, Jerome Landrieu, Richard Cusick
Coordinator: Dora Gonzales

ASIA

CHINA

Barry Callebaut Suzhou Chocolate Co, Ltd, 138 Fangzhong Street, Suzhou Industrial Park, Suzhou, 215024
Tel: +86-512-62.89.01.09
Fax: +86-512-62890178
Technical Advisor: Jean-Marc Bernelin
Coordinator: Willa Shao

INDIA

Barry Callebaut India Pvt. Ltd., # 401, 4th Floor, Times Square, Western Express Highway, Adheri East, 400069, Mumbai
Tel: +91-226-721.30.80, Fax: +91-226-721.30.99
Technical Advisor: Abihiru Biswas
Coordinator: Arlene D Souza

MALAYSIA

Lot 2, Lebuh Sultan Mohamed 1 - Bandar Sultan Suleiman 4200 Port Klang - Selangor Dural Ehsan Malaysia
Tel: + 603 3169 3333
Fax: + 603 3176 2948

RUSSIAN FEDERATION

Barry Callebaut NL Russia LLC, Industrial building, Near Chepelevo village, Rural settlement Stremilovskoe, Chekhov district, 142301 Moscow region
Tel: +7 499 922 19 30, Fax: +7 499 922 19 31
Technical Advisor: Eduard Lebedev

THE WORLD CHOCOLATE MASTERS

THIS COMPETITION HAS BECOME THE ULTIMATE AMBITION FOR CHOCOLATIERS WORLDWIDE, AND THE CULMINATION OF EXCELLENCE IN THE WORLD OF CHOCOLATE. THE 2011 WORLD FINAL TAKES PLACE IN PARIS FROM OCTOBER 19TH TO 21ST, WITH PRESELECTION OF NATIONAL CANDIDATES FROM MAY TO AUGUST, 2011.

The origins of the competition come from the merger in 2004 of two original events: 'Le Grand Prix International de la Chocolaterie' organised in France by Cacao Barry, and the 'International Belgium Chocolate Award' organised by Callebaut. Although the two companies had come together in 1996, the competitions were separate until the merger, and the first joint competition was held in 2005.

The Masters takes place every two years and one of its great strengths is in its preselection of candidates. Individual nations hold internal competitions to field suitable candidates, and these are selected – just one from each nation – to go forward to the world final. The judges are not just looking for creative designs, but also technical skills and, above all, the taste of the finished product.

Each year the Masters gives candidates a theme. In 2009 it was 'haute couture' and the winner was Shigeo Hirai, the sous-chef of the Grand Hyatt Tokyo, with an astonishing 'sculpture' of a girl model in full hat, gloves, gown and shoes.

The theme for 2011 is 'Cocoa – Quetzalcoatl's Gift' – the origins of chocolate, of course, are in equatorial central and south America, and the Aztecs believed that the god Quetzalcoatl had given mankind cocoa as a gift to provide relaxation and pleasure. The brief is that all the items prepared in the final should recall the original discovery of cocoa, as well as reflecting the tastes and flavours of central America. The history is certainly colourful and should provide considerable inspiration for the finalists:

An Aztec legend tells of a princess who is left to watch over a great treasure belonging to her husband who has gone off to defend the borders of the empire. While he is away, she is attacked by his enemies who try in vain to make her reveal the place where the treasure is hidden. As revenge for her silence they kill her and from her blood springs the cocoa plant whose fruit hid a treasure in its seeds, which were as bitter as the sufferings of love, as strong as virtue and as red as blood. Cocoa was Quetzalcoatl's gift for the woman's faithfulness to her husband even unto death.

WORLD CHOCOLATE MASTERS

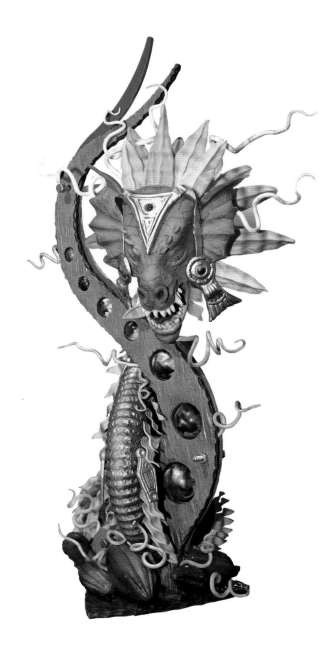

In the national preselections, competitors have 15 hours (seven hours on day one, eight hours on day two) to complete their tasks in front of a live audience:

1) Chocolate showpiece – on the Quetzalcoatl theme, between one and two metres high.

2) Dipped praline – minimum 50 pieces of at least 15 grammes each.

3) Moulded praline – minimum 50 pieces of at least 15 grammes each.

4) Chocolate pastry – two identical chocolate layered cakes for eight people.

5) Gastronomic Chocolate Dessert – chocolate dessert with at least four textures to serve six.

6) 'Mystery Box' assignment – details to be revealed on the day.

In the final the contestants have 11½ hours (three hours on day one, eight and a half hours on day two) to complete their tasks in front of a live audience:

1) Chocolate showpiece – on the Quetzalcoatl theme, between one and two metres high.

2) Dipped praline – minimum 48 pieces of at least 15 grammes each.

3) Moulded praline – minimum 48 pieces of at least 15 grammes each.

4) Chocolate pastry – two identical chocolate layered cakes for eight people

5) Gastronomic Chocolate Dessert – chocolate dessert with at least four textures to serve six.

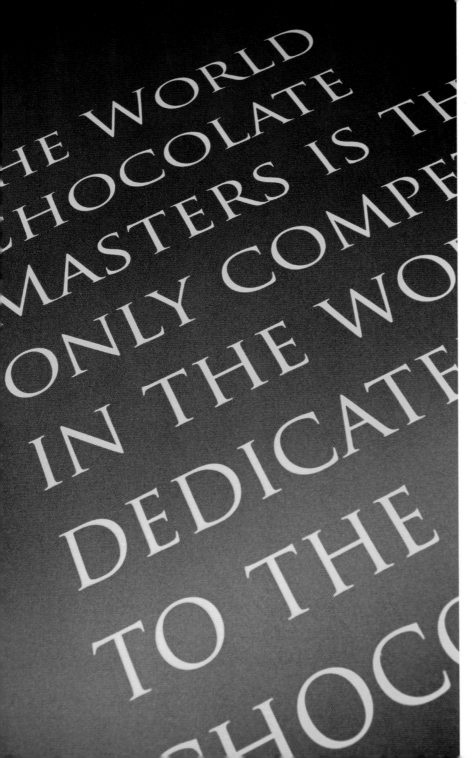

THE NATIONAL FINALISTS WHO
WILL GO FORWARD TO THE
WORLD FINAL ARE AS FOLLOWS:

AUSTRALIA

Seung Yun Lee
Savour Chocolate & Patisserie School,
Melbourne

BELGIUM

Ryan Stevenson
Pâtissier at 'Le Saint Aulaye' in Ixelles

CANADA

Véronique Rousseau
Chocolatière at Choco Daisy in
Drummondville

DENMARK

Palle Sørensen
Pastry Chef at Langenæs Bageri in Aarhus

EASTERN EUROPE

Mariusz Buritta
Pâtissier at Sowa Pâtisserie, Poland

FRANCE

Xavier Berger
Chocolatier and owner of Berger
chocolatier in Tarbes, France

GERMANY

Jana Ristau
Confectioner at Törtchen törtchen,
Cologne

ICELAND

Asgeir Sandholt
Sandholt Bakery, Reykjavik

ITALY

Yumiko Saimura
Piccola Pasticceria, Casale Monferrato

JAPAN

Yoshiaki Uezaki
Pâtisserie Kosai, Mito

LEBANON

Damien Deslandes
Faqra Catering, Beirut

MEXICO

Luis Robledo
Consorcio Icon, México city

NETHERLANDS

Frank Haasnoot
Executive Pastry Chef at Dobla, Alkmaar

RUSSIA

Aleksander Ilyukhin
Pastry-chef of bakery chain 'Le Khleb',
Russia

SPAIN

Francisco José Somoza Estévez
Best Spanish Pastry Chef 2007 in Madrid

SWITZERLAND

Claudia Schmid
Confiserie Sprüngli, Zurich

TAIWAN

Chi Hsien Cheng
Le Meridien Taipei Hotel, Taipei

UNITED KINGDOM

John Costello
Park Cakes, Oldham

USA

Sylvain Bortolini
Bellagio resort, Las Vegas

Although the event is a wonderful piece of theatre and entertainment, the value it gives to the industry is immeasurable. Young craftsmen and craftswomen are encouraged to allow their creativity to run free, and to be selected for the final is a wonderful attribute to add to the contestants' qualifications, with the winner open to an a number of exclusive opportunities.

The 2009 winner, Shigeo Hirai, was quoted as saying that during the run-up to the final "I met chefs who I had only known through pictures", and that "the competition itself was a gigantic but amusing event: it stimulated me and I can still feel the excitement. It surely was the experience of my life." In October, 2011 one of the national finalists will be sharing that experience, while for the first time the 2011 event will be streamed live on the internet.

WINNING WITH CHOCOLATE

CURRENT REIGNING CHAMPIONS OF THE WORLD CHOCOLATE MASTERS ARE JAPAN – WITH THE COUNTRY WINNING THE COVETED AWARD IN THE LAST TWO COMPETITIONS. NOW WELL KNOWN AS CHOCOLATE LEADERS WITH THEIR INGENIOUS BLEND OF FLAVOUR, TEXTURES AND AESTHETICALLY PLEASING CREATIONS JAPAN ARE STRONG COMPETITION FOR ANOTHER YEAR AT THE TOP OF THE WORLD CHOCOLATE MASTERS AWARDS.

Winning the competition in 2007, Naomi Mizuno was crowned the World Chocolate Master in a competition that took place at the Salon du Chocolat Professional held in Paris. Naomi proved his skills around a theme of 'National Myths and Legends' and was faced with a judging panel of experts including Spanish master chocolatier Francisco Torreblanca. The Japanese entrant wowed the judges with his chocolate pastry and his amazing showpiece. As well as winning a number of prizes Naomi is now a designated Callebaut ambassador.

Following in suit, Japanese contestant Shigeo Hirai won the competition in 2009, making Japan World Chocolate Master champions for two consecutive competitions. Again the competition, held at the Salon du Chocolat Professional in Paris attracted enthusiasts from around the globe, and with mouthwatering cakes and stylish desserts Shigeo didn't disappoint. Following the theme of 'Haute Couture' the Japanese entrant shone with his chic lady showpiece while his creative hat of buttons attracted many wanton glances.

Perhaps not an obvious winner as countries with stronger chocolate roots, the patience, passion and concentration that has been shown from the Japanese contestants make the country a very worthy winner. Although highly credited in all areas of the competition, the

clear strength of both Naomi Mizuno and Shigeo Hirai's entries has been the complicated and fascinated showpieces. Never failing to stun crowds and jury's alike, both showpieces offer a unique and highly creative chocolate creation.

Now with the whole world watching, can Japan's 2011 World Chocolate Master contestant Yoshiaki Uezaki win this year to make it a hat-trick for Japan? With 17 other worthy contestants, this competition is set to be the most exciting event yet!

"THE CLEAR STRENGTH OF
BOTH NAOMI MIZUNO AND
SHIGEO HIRAI'S ENTRIES HAS
BEEN THE COMPLICATED AND
FASCINATED SHOWPIECES."

WCM WINNER 2009

SHIGEO HIRAI

JAPAN, 2009

SHIGEO HIRAI

Shigeo Hirai was crowned winner of the World Chocolate Masters 2009 – wowing judges with his creative take on chocolate haute couture. A graduate of Tsuji Cooking Academy Shigeo grew up in Hyogo prefecture and travelled to France to develop his skills before returning to Japan. Having taken part in many competitions including 2nd prize for chocolate at the Japan-selection of 'coupe de Monde', Shigeo is now vice president chef of pastry at the Grand Hyatt hotel Tokyo.

WCM WINNER 2007

NAOMI MIZUNO

JAPAN, 2007

NAOMI MIZUNO

For Naomi Mizuno pâtisserie has always been a way of life – having worked in a number of locations in both Japan and France he has earned a great deal of experience along the way. Now Naomi works at Pâtisserie Mountain, in Kyoto his own shop that he has taken over from his father. Naomi has taken part in many competitions including winning the World Chocolate Masters in 2007 and was designated as a Callebaut ambassador in 2008.

AUSTRALIA

DESPITE ITS DEADLY CREATURES, AUSTRALIA IS THE IDEAL PLACE FOR THOSE WHO LOVE THE OUTDOORS AND EXPLORING THE UNKNOWN.

With big cities such as Canberra, Darwin, Adelaide and Perth there is plenty to keep the visitor occupied, particularly for those who enjoy a good cultural atmosphere. Australia is renowned for its surfing beaches which frame the coast. North of Brisbane, visitors will find glittering beaches along the beautiful Sunshine Coast and south of Brisbane is the Gold Coast, where Australia's sun-seekers flock. In the south, the great city of Melbourne, with a thriving arts scene and a passion for fine dining is a must-visit, not to mention the tourist's dream — the city of Sydney. To truly dive into the realms of Australian lifestyle then experience Whitsunday Islands, surrounded by natural beauty and blue-green waterways. Australia is most certainly a place to be discovered.

Chocolate was first introduced to Australia in 1914, with Ernest Hillier as the first chocolate manufacturer making premium quality chocolates. Prior to this, the only way for Australia to experience the luxury of chocolate was through it being imported from overseas. Following on from this in 1915, Haigh's chocolate manufacturer was established and is classed as Australia's oldest manufacturer.

"IN 1915, HAIGH'S CHOCOLATE MANUFACTURER WAS ESTABLISHED AND IS CLASSED AS AUSTRALIA'S OLDEST MANUFACTURER."

WINNER

SEUNG YUN LEE

AUSTRALIA

SEUNG YUN LEE

Having started her career in graphic design Seung Yun Lee was inspired by the film 'Chocolat' and decided to work in an area where she could explore her creativity. Having worked previously in Korea she moved to Australia where she started working for Savour Chocolate & Pâtisserie School where she is now a pastry chef. Having received several awards through Barry Callebaut competitions in Australia, she was awarded first place for the 2010 Callebaut Easter Egg Challenge and is also the winner of the 2010 World Chocolate Masters Australia pre-selection.

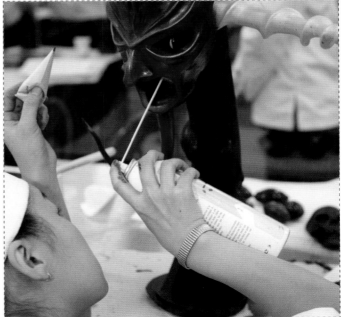

BREATHE OF QUETZALCOATL

COATED PRALINE, BY SEUNG YUN LEE MAKES 75

INGREDIENTS

NIBS PRALINE

187g Caster sugar
125g Callebaut cocoa nibs
1 Vanilla bean
1g Salt

TEQUILA SUGAR CRUST

Corn starch, for the moulds
250g Caster sugar
100g Water
75g Tequila

LEMON GANACHE

115g Fresh cream 35%
11g Liquid glucose
5g Sorbitol liquid
38g Callebaut Madagascar 67% Origine
306g Cacao Barry Ghana 40% Origine
50g Lemon juice
5g Lemon zest
8g Butter

Cacao Barry Ghana 40% Origine, to coat

PROCESS

NIBS PRALINE

Preheat a saucepan over a medium heat, add the sugar one-third at a time to make dry caramel. Once melted, ensuring there are no lumps add all the other ingredients and mix. When fully mixed and melted spread on a silpat mat and leave to cool. When cool break into pieces and put it in the Robotcoupe to make a praline. Spread 2mm high in a plastic frame.

TEQUILA SUGAR CRUST

Warm the starch around 60°C in the oven, press into the starch with prepared moulds and continue to keep warm until needed. Meanwhile boil together the sugar and water to 116°C. Warm up a stainless steel bowl and pour the sugar mixture into it then pour the Tequila into the warm saucepan, then add the warmed alcohol over the sugar. Pour this mixture back into the saucepan and repeat the process back and forth three times. Pour this mix it into a depositor and fill the starch moulds. Cover the liqueur with sifted starch and leave for three hours then cover with a lid and flip the tray over leave for at least another three hours. Brush the excess starch away.

LEMON GANACHE

Boil the cream with the glucose and the sorbitol. Pour the hot cream on the half melted dark and milk couverture and mix to obtain a smooth emulsion. Heat the lemon juice and zest to 40°C and strain through a fine chinois. Add the juice a little at a time to the ganache. Cool slightly and add the butter at 38°C. Pour onto the nibs praline.

ASSEMBLY

Dip the filling in Cacao Barry Ghana 40% Origine and decorate.

AZTEC PYRAMID

MOULDED PRALINE, BY SEUNG YUN LEE MAKES 75

INGREDIENTS

CRUNCHY BASE

50g Callebaut Arriba 39% Origine
100g Callebaut Hazelnut Praline 50%
15g Callebaut Mycryo
50g Callebaut Paillete Feuilletine

CITRUS GANACHE

150g Honey
100g Orange juice
Zest of 1 orange
60g Pineapple, chopped
3g Cinnamon stick
1 Star anise
1 Vanilla pod
10g Mambo rum
24g Butter
4g Lemon thyme
150g Cream
18g Invert sugar
38g Sugar
200g Callebaut Arriba 39% Origine
100g Callebaut Madagascar 67% Origine
60g Butter

Cacao Barry Extra Bitter Guayaquil, to coat

PROCESS

CRUNCHY BASE

Mix all the ingredients together except
the paillete feuilletine. Crystallize the mix
in the microwave until it melts, around
30°C. Mix really well and add the Paillete
feuilletine. Spread onto a silicon sheet and
cut into squares 2 x 2cm and chill.

CITRUS GANACHE

To make a citrus essence boil together
the honey, orange juice, zest, pineapple,
cinnamon, star anise and vanilla bean.
Once it has boiled reduce the heat and
simmer to reduce to 200g and pass
through a sieve. Add the rum and mix well.
Boil the 24g of butter, lemon thyme,
cream, invert sugar and the sugar, infuse
for 10 minutes then sieve and boil with
the citrus essence. When boiled add the
chocolates and mix, then add in the butter
and mix.

ASSEMBLY

Coat the mould with Cacao Barry Extra
Bitter Guayaquil and chill, then fill with
the ganache and finish with the crunchy
base. Coat with more Guayaquil.

WORLD CHOCOLATE MASTERS 2011

WIND OF QUETZALCOATLS

PLATED DESSERT, BY SEUNG YUN LEE SERVES 6

INGREDIENTS

HAZELNUT DACQUAISE

108g Egg white
34g Caster sugar
97g Icing sugar
97g Hazelnut powder
100g Hazelnuts, halved

ORANGE CHOCOLATE CREAM

Zest of 1 Orange
332g Fresh Cream 35%
382g Callebaut Arriba 39% Origin
5g Grand Marnier

CITRUS CHOCOLATE EGG

100g Blood orange purée
100g Mandarin purée
50g Blackberry purée
1g Xantana

SKIN

200g Callebaut Cocoa Butter
200g Callebaut Arriba 39% Origine

MILK CHOCOLATE CHANTILLY

283g Fresh cream 35%
200g Callebaut Arriba 39% origin

NIBS & COCOA BUTTER

25g Callebaut cocoa butter
75g Callebaut cocoa nibs

CHOCOLATE SORBET

1000g Semi-skimmed milk
60g Invert sugar
60g Callebaut cocoa powder
340g Callebaut Java 33% Origine

CHOCOLATE CARAMEL TUILES

100g Liquid glucose
100g Fondant
45g Callebaut cocoa mass

CHILLI & LIME WARM CHOCOLATE

25g Fresh chilli
25g Lime oil
500g Cacao Barry 66% Mexique Origine

PROCESS

HAZELNUT DACQUAISE

Sift the dry ingredients. Make a meringue with egg white and sugar. Mix with icing sugar and hazelnut powder and pour into flexipan 1cm high. Sprinkle halved hazelnuts on the top. Bake in the oven 190°C for 15-20 minutes.

ORANGE CHOCOLATE CREAM

Infuse orange zest in the boiled cream for 10 minutes. Sieve through to the Arriba milk chocolate and mix. Leave to cool to room temperature and add the Grand Marnier and mix.

CITRUS CHOCOLATE EGG

Warm all the purées together over a low heat just to warm the mix then stir in Xantana combine with an emersion blender. Pour in to half-sphere flexipan moulds and freeze.

SKIN

Melt all the ingredients together and then dip the citrus chocolate egg to coat.

MILK CHOCOLATE CHANTILLY

Boil the cream pour onto Arriba chocolate cover and leave it in the fridge for 5 hours then whip.

NIBS & COCOA BUTTER

Melt the cocoa butter in small saucepan over a low heat. Add nibs and cook for 1 minute, leave to cool on a paper towel.

CHOCOLATE SORBET

Boil and then simmer the milk, invert sugar and cocoa powder for 10 minutes. Sieve this onto Java milk chocolate. Cool and churn in an ice cream machine following manufacturer's instructions.

CHOCOLATE CARAMEL TUILES

Boil the glucose and fondant to 163°C, and then add the cocoa mass mix and leave to cool. Spread a thin layer on a silpat mat. Put it in pre-heated oven 150°C for 10 minutes.

CHILLI & LIME WARM CHOCOLATE

Infuse the chilli in the lime oil, then mix 2 teaspoons of the oil with 500g tempered Mexique dark chocolate.

ASSEMBLY

Fill a chocolate cylinder on a plate with the dacquoise, then add the orange chocolate cream, then the citrus chocolate egg and finally cover with chantilly cream. Sprinkle the nibs on top of the cylinder and add a quenelle of sorbet. Next to the cylinder secure the caramel tuile with chilli and lime chocolate so that it leans against the cylinder. Decorate the plate with airbrushed chocolate.

AZTEC GIFTS

ENTREMET, BY SEUNG YUN LEE SERVES 8

INGREDIENTS

COCOA NIBS SABLE

160g Butter
165g Icing sugar
2g Salt
15g Egg yolks
230g Flour
40g Callebaut cocoa powder
10g Baking powder
30g Callebaut cocoa nibs
Callebaut Mycryo, for dusting

PINEAPPLE WITH SPICE

1 Pineapple, chopped
1 Orange
150g Brown sugar
25g Mambo rum
1 Vanilla bean
1 Cinnamon stick
1 Star anise

AZTEC HOT CHOCOLATE JELLY

40g Callebaut cocoa powder
550g Water
8g Cinnamon powder
240g Honey
4g Agar agar
40g Butterscotch

MILK CHOCOLATE ORANGE CREAM

332g Fresh Cream 35%
Zest of 1 orange
382g Callebaut Arriba 39% Origine
5g Grand Marnier

CHOCOLATE SPONGE

95g Callebaut cocoa powder
135g Plain flour
285g Egg yolks
240g Caster sugar
55g Caster sugar
275g Egg whites
1 pinch Cream of tartar
95g Butter, melted but not hot

GRAND MARNIER SYRUP

100g Water
100g Caster Sugar
20g Grand Marnier

WHITE CHOCOLATE MOUSSE

150g Fresh cream 35%
6g Gold gelatine sheets
285g Blanc Satin (Cacao Barry)
375g Fresh cream 35%, semi-whipped

CHOCOLATE GLAZE

250g Water
600g Caster sugar
400g Fresh cream 35%
250g Cocoa powder (Cacao Barry)
200g Liquid glucose
27g Gold gelatine sheets

PROCESS

COCOA NIBS SABLE

Beat the softened butter with the icing sugar and salt. Once light add the egg yolks, and then add the flour, cocoa powder and baking powder. Once mixed add the cocoa nibs. Bake at 170°C for approximately 10 minutes. Once baked sieve some Mycryo on the top and leave to cool.

PINEAPPLE WITH SPICE

Mix everything together in a saucepan and cook on a low/medium heat until golden brown.

AZTEC HOT CHOCOLATE JELLY

Boil all together except the butterscotch until Agar Agar strips have melted. Sieve and add the butterscotch. Pour into a 18cm flexipan and put it in the fridge to set.

MILK CHOCOLATE ORANGE CREAM

Boil the cream and orange zest then pour over the milk chocolate. Whisk and once all the chocolate is melted add Grand Marnier.

CHOCOLATE SPONGE

Sieve together the cocoa powder and flour. Mix together egg yolks and 240g caster sugar and make a stiff peak meringue with egg white, the 55g caster sugar and pinch of cream of tartar. Mix the egg yolk mixture with the dry ingredients and then together with the meringue mix. Pour to 1cm high in a 16cm flexipan. Bake 10 minutes at 170°C.

GRAND MARNIER SYRUP

Boil the water and sugar and then add the Grand Marnier.

WHITE CHOCOLATE MOUSSE

Boil the 150g cream and then add the pre-soaked gelatine and pour onto the half-melted white chocolate. Fold through the remaining 375g cream and chill.

CHOCOLATE GLAZE

Boil the water with the sugar to 110°C. Then add the cream, cocoa powder and glucose reboil it. Mix with an emersion blender and then sieve, then add the pre soaked gelatine. Allow to cool at room temperature before coating the entremets.

ASSEMBLY

Prepare 16cm x 3.5cm high cake ring by placing an acetate strip around inside the ring. Add the layers of cocoa nib sable, then the pineapple, then the chocolate jelly, the chocolate orange cream and finally the sponge soaked in some of the syrup. Freeze and then unmould it. Prepare a 18cm x 4.5cm high cake ring with acetate strip around the inside of the ring and place the cake inside it, pour the white chocolate mousse around and over the cake and freeze. Remove from the ring and coat with glaze and decorate.

BELGIUM

BELGIUM, IT SEEMS HAS FINALLY COME OF AGE – CONSIDERED AS ONE OF EUROPE'S MOST UNDER-RATED DESTINATIONS IT'S MORE THAN JUST WAFFLES AND E.U. BUREAUCRACY.

The dynamic capital city of Brussels, provides a vibrant atmosphere which is big on café living and Art Nouveau. While Antwerp, second largest city and municipality in Belgium as well as the capital city of the province of Flanders, is renowned for its fascinating architecture and historical institutions. Bruges is somewhat similar, full of artistic treasures and more than its fair share of imposing historic monuments ensures it is considered one of the gems of northwest Europe.

The country itself has a population of about 10.8 million people and is split into two sections – Flanders, the predominantly Dutch-speaking north and Wallonia, the predominantly French-speaking south. When it comes to chocolate Belgium is world famous and at the forefront of the business, boasting over 2000 chocolate shops and countless opportunities to see how such marvels are created. What makes Belgium chocolate so unique is that it is still made by hand in small shops using original equipment.

"WHEN IT COMES TO CHOCOLATE BELGIUM IS WORLD FAMOUS AND AT THE FOREFRONT OF THE BUSINESS."

WINNER

RYAN STEVENSON

BELGIUM

RYAN STEVENSON

A second time winner of the Belgian heats, Australian Ryan Stevenson is famed for winning the trophy for 'Best Praline' in the 2009 World Chocolate Masters competition. Since the last competition, Ryan has gained much experience particularly at home and in the world of chocolate and is currently a pâtissier at Le Saint Aulaye in Brussels. Ryan has worked in Australia, UK and taken part in many competitions and hopes to improve his skills further by participating in the World Chocolate Masters 2011.

SECOND PLACE

PHILLIPPE LAFONT

At SFSME Institute in Brussels, Philippe Lafont is the training manager for bakery, pastry and chocolate. A versatile craftsman who loves to share his knowledge Phillippe is always looking for innovation and perfection which is clearly shown in his work. Previously Phillippe has worked for 'Pastry Arnould' so he has a great deal of experience in this field.

THIRD PLACE

NICOLAS ARNAUD

A pastry chef from Brussels with an international story – after his studies in France, Nicolas has worked in England and finally returned to Brussels to work at Pastry Fabrice Collignon and now the vast Pastry Ducobu in Waterloo. Nicolas is enthusiastic about chocolate and sees the competition as a great place for chefs to meet to discuss their passion.

AU CŒUR D'AMOUR (CENTRE OF LOVE)

COATED PRALINE, BY RYAN STEVENSON MAKES 250

INGREDIENTS

PINE NUT PRALINE

60g Water
170g Sugar
300g Pine nuts
20g Sesame seeds
6g Lemon zest
½ Vanilla bean
2g Salt

LAVENDER GANACHE

340g Cream
25g Glucose
6g Lavender
40g Trimoline
375g Ghanaian dark chocolate
300g Arriba milk chocolate

Callebaut 835 with 5% extra cocoa butter
added, to cover

PROCESS

PINE NUT PRALINE

Heat the sugar and water to 121°C, then
add the pine nuts and sesame. Cook until a
light caramel forms. Cool and put through
the food processor with the lemon zest,
vanilla and salt.

LAVENDER GANACHE

Boil the cream with the glucose, lavender
and trimoline. Infuse for 30 minutes.
Heat the chocolates, add the liquid and
emulsify.

ASSEMBLY

Pour the ganache into a frame. Put 300g
pine nut praline mixed with 130g of Arriba
milk chocolate on top and underneath the
ganache which is already crystallised. Coat
with Callebaut 835 with 5% extra cocoa
butter added.

MORCEAU DE SOLEIL (PIECE OF SUN)

MOULDED PRALINE, BY RYAN STEVENSON MAKES 75

INGREDIENTS

CARAMEL WITH PASSIONFRUIT & FRESH THYME

4g Fresh thyme
50g Cream
30g Glucose
80g Sugar
40g Passionfruit purée
15g Mango purée
75g Arriba milk chocolate

YOGHURT GANACHE

40g Cream
70g Yoghurt
7g Trimoline
55g Sao Thome dark chocolate
115g Arriba milk chocolate

Callebaut 835 chocolate, to coat

PROCESS

CARAMEL WITH PASSIONFRUIT & FRESH THYME

Infuse the fresh thyme with the cream and glucose for 30 minutes. Make a light caramel with the sugar, add the cream, then the purées and finish with the chocolate.

YOGHURT GANACHE

Heat the cream with the yoghurt and trimoline, add the chocolates and emulsify.

ASSEMBLY

Spray demi-sphere moulds with black cocoa butter and then coat using Callebaut 835. Fill the moulds with the caramel first and then the ganache. When the ganache is firm, close the moulds with Callebaut 835. Decorate with a small chocolate diamond piece.

LA VOYAGE DE DECOUVRIR (THE VOYAGE OF DISCOVERY)

PLATED DESSERT, BY RYAN STEVENSON SERVES 6

INGREDIENTS

BROWNIES

55g Madirofolo dark chocolate
50g Butter
30g Sugar
15g Flour
40g Almond flour 100%
25g Brown sugar
1 Egg

PEACH & BANANA SET COULIS

150g Peaches
50g Banana
80g Sugar syrup
40g Trimoline
6g Pectin NH
10g Sugar
40g Passionfruit purée
40g Apricot purée

CHOCOLATE CREAM

165g Milk
30g Cream
10g Glucose
30g Sugar
35g Egg yolks
12g Cornstarch
50g Dark chocolate 811
45g Sao Thomé dark chocolate
15g Butter

CHOCOLATE FOAM

300g Chocolate cream
50g Cream
150g Milk

FERMENTED POMEGRANATE ICE CREAM

200g Milk
50g Cream
70g Sugar
120g Egg yolks
2g Stabiliser
150g Pomegranate purée
½ Vanilla pod
100g Fermented pomegranate

CHOCOLATE TUILE

300g Fondant
200g Glucose
200g Arriba milk chocolate

PEACH AND BANANA COULIS

150g Peach and banana set coulis
60g Peaches
40g Banana

VANILLA MERINGUE

170g Egg whites
170g Sugar
½ Vanilla pod

PROCESS

BROWNIES

Mix everything together, fill the moulds and bake at 150°C for 10 minutes.

PEACH & BANANA SET COULIS

Mix the fruit together with the sugar syrup, then cook with the trimoline and pectin already mixed with the sugar. Boil and add the purées and pour over the brownies.

CHOCOLATE CREAM

Make a crème patissère with the milk, cream, glucose, sugar, egg yolks and cornstarch. Add the chocolates and butter, mix and cool.

CHOCOLATE FOAM

Mix together all ingredients then pour into siphon and add two gas charges.

FERMENTED POMEGRANATE ICE CREAM

Make a crème Anglaise with the milk, cream, sugar, egg yolks and stabiliser. Add the purée and then freeze.

CHOCOLATE TUILE

Cook the fondant and glucose at 150°C. Add the chocolate.

PEACH AND BANANA COULIS

Mix together the set coulis with the fruit purées and set aside.

VANILLA MERINGUE

Make a meringue with all the ingredients, fill the moulds and bake at 150°C for 15 minutes. When cool, makes a small round hole inside the meringue.

ASSEMBLY

Take the chocolate brownies with the peach and banana set coulis on top and place on assiette. Using the siphon, add the chocolate foam. Take a small spoon and scoop the fermented pomegranate ice cream and place into the meringue. Add the meringue on top of the chocolate foam. Take a piece of chocolate tuile, and place on top of the meringue. Heat using a blowtorch until the tuille has melted and taken on the form of the meringue. Add the peach and banana coulis onto the plate and serve.

'TONATIUH' THE WARRIOR SUN GOD

ENTREMET, BY RYAN STEVENSON MAKES 2 CAKES, EACH SERVES 8

INGREDIENTS

BISCUIT (FLOUR-FREE)

130g Egg yolks
40g Ground almonds
40g Sugar
20g Cocoa powder
168g Egg whites
90g Sugar

CRUMBLE

190g Crumble
190g Sugar
160g Flour
150g Butter
6g Salt
8g Orange zest
½ Vanilla pod

MASCARPONE WITH PECAN NUTS

1 Gelatine sheet
30g Cream
10g Icing sugar
120g Mascarpone
50g Mascarpone with pecan nuts

BLOOD ORANGE COULIS

3 Gelatine sheets
50g Trimoline
250g Unsweetened blood orange juice
60g Orange concentrate

CRISP

250g Crumble
100g Chocolate 811
50g Mascarpone with pecan nuts

CHOCOLATE MOUSSE

170g Milk
60g Cream
45g Egg yolks
20g Trimoline
225g Madirofolo chocolate
60g Arriba milk chocolate
320g Whipped cream

CHOCOLATE ICING

150g Milk
75g Cream
100g Glucose
250g Brilliance
350g Dark chocolate 811

RUSSIAN TARTINE

60g Butter
20g Brown sugar
65g Flour
40g Sugar
1g Salt

PROCESS

BISCUIT (FLOUR-FREE)

Beat the egg yolks, add the sifted dry ingredients. Beat the egg whites with the sugar and mix the two together well.

CRUMBLE

Mix all the ingredients and then cool and grate. Cook on a silpat at 150°C for 25 minutes.

MASCARPONE WITH PECAN NUTS

Melt the gelatine in the cream, add the icing sugar and then the remaining ingredients.

BLOOD ORANGE COULIS

Melt the gelatine with the trimoline and 50g of juice. Add the remaining ingredients and chill to make 90g inserts.

CRISP

Mix everything together and cook on a silpat at 170°C for 25 minutes.

CHOCOLATE MOUSSE

Make a crème Anglaise with the milk, cream, egg yolks and trimoline. Mix well and pour over the chocolates. Add the whipped cream when the mixture gets to 40°C.

CHOCOLATE ICING

Boil the milk, cream and the glucose together. Pour over the chocolates, mix and use at 45°C.

RUSSIAN TARTINE

Mix everything together and then roll out to 1mm. Bake at 170°C for 15 minutes and then cut into squares.

ASSEMBLY

In a 16cm cake ring add a layer of biscuit, on top of this add a layer of crumble then a layer of mascarpone and leave to chill before adding a layer of coulis. On top of the coulis add a layer of crisp and then chill. Remove from the frame and place in a 18cm cake ring. Cover all sides with the chocolate mousse and then freeze. When frozen remove from the tin and coat with icing, place Russian tartine squares around the edge to decorate.

DENMARK

SITUATED IN NORTHERN EUROPE, DENMARK IS THE SMALLEST SCANDINAVIAN COUNTRY AND A PLACE WHERE RURAL AND URBAN COME TOGETHER TO COMBINE ANCIENT RUINS AND MODERN DESIGNS.

With everything in close proximity, Denmark allows for visitors to combine both the buzz of the city and the tranquility of the countryside. No matter where you are, sandy beaches and beautiful green forests are only a 30 minute drive away. Taking a trip to Copenhagen, visitors can experience fine dining since Copenhagen's restaurants have more Michelin stars than any other Scandinavian city.

Copenhagen is also at the heart of chocolate indulgence where there is an ever growing need to produce the finest chocolate. It's important to note that chocolatiers are hard to find in Copenhagen, however they must not be overlooked as on discovery visitors will find that they incorporate the skills and traditions of Europe's best chocolatiers but with a contemporary experimental twist. This experimental twist makes it well worth a visit.

"COPENHAGEN IS ALSO AT THE HEART OF CHOCOLATE INDULGENCE WHERE THERE IS AN EVER GROWING NEED TO PRODUCE THE FINEST CHOCOLATE."

WINNER

PALLE SØRENSEN

DENMARK

PALLE SØRENSEN

Second place in the Scandinavia pre-selection went to Palle Sørensen from Denmark who goes through as the finalist from Denmark. Since 1999 Palle has worked as a chef at institutions such as Schweizerbageriet, Hjertebageriet, Harlev bageriet and Langenæsbageriet. He has also won a number of awards and competitions, and competed in Italy and Germany. A determined chocolatier, he is passionate about becoming World Chocolate Master 2011.

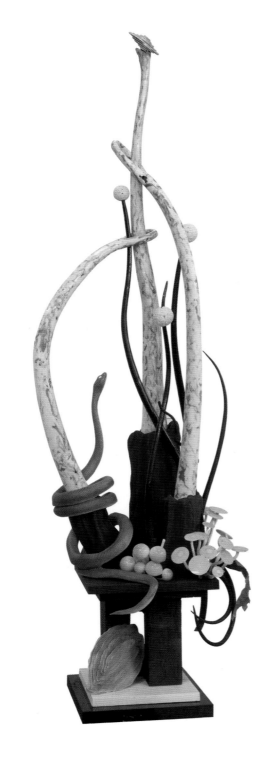

WILDERNESS

COATED PRALINE, BY PALLE SØRENSEN MAKES 40

INGREDIENTS

MEXIQUE TRUFFLE

200g Fresh cream
100 Glucose
120g Alto El Sol 65% (Cacao Barry)
105g Mexique 66% (Cacao Barry)
40g Organic smoked butter

PUFFED PORK RINDS

30g Pork rind granules
Coconut oil, to fry
1.1g Mayan Sun gourmet sea salt, crushed
25g Caramelised Brazil nuts, crushed

AMBRA TRUFFLE

125g Fresh cream
60g Glucose
264g Ambra 36% (Cacao Barry), broken
25g Butter

12g Blanc Satin 29.2%, to coat
88g Tanzanie 75%, to coat

PROCESS

THE MEXIQUE TRUFFLE

Boil the cream together with the glucose. Gently pour it over the broken chocolate, a little at a time while stirring. At 29-30°C add the organic smoked butter with the cocoa beans.

PUFFED PORK RINDS

Fry the granules of pork rinds in coconut oil. Mix with the crushed Mayan Sun gourmet sea salt and the crushed caramelised Brazil nuts.

AMBRA TRUFFLE

Heat the cream and glucose until it boils. Gently pour it over the chopped chocolate a little at a time. Cool to 29-30°C then add the softened butter and mix.

ASSEMBLY

Place the dark Mexique truffle in the bottom a tin. In the middle put the puffed pork rinds, the gourmet salt and the caramelised Brazil nuts. Then layer the light Ambra truffle on top. Let it rest for 48 hours at 14-16°C.

Divide it into pieces that are 1.6 x 3.5cm, approximately 1cm high. Immerse the pieces in a mixture of Blanc Satin and Tanzanie. Decorate with Mayan Sun gourmet sea salt, choco nibs, dried vanilla corn and 3D plastic with bronze.

XITOMATL

MOULDED PRALINE, BY PALLE SØRENSEN MAKES 40

INGREDIENTS

TOMATO TRUFFLE

380g Cream
325g Glucose
445g Madagascar 67% (Callebaut)
86g Butter
32g Freeze-dried tomato
1.5g Gourmet salt

Blanc Satin 29.2% (Cacao Barry), to coat
Tanzanie 75% (Cacao Barry), to coat

PROCESS

TOMATO TRUFFLE

Boil the cream and glucose together. Pour
it a little at a time over the Madagascar
chocolate while stirring. After an emulsion
is made add the softened butter. Add the
tomato and salt and mix well.

ASSEMBLY

Coat the moulds in a mixture of 12%
Blanc Satin and 88% Tanzanie and then
fill with the tomato truffle, leave to cool
and then close.

DISCOVERY

PLATED DESSERT, BY PALLE SØRENSEN SERVES 6

INGREDIENTS

MAGNA CAKE

70g Organic whole milk
80g Organic sugar
175g Tanzanie 75% (Cacao Barry)
100g Organic butter
140g Pasteurised egg whites
130g Pasteurised egg yolks
40g Organic flour
12g Cocoa
0.75g Gourmet salt

AVOCADO ICE CREAM

200g Condensed milk
150g Sparkling mineral water
110g Organic sugar
½ Thaiti vanilla pod
150g Organic cream
80g Organic egg yolks
155g Madagascar 67% (Callebaut)
100g Avocado
26g Organic lime juice

WHITE CHOCOLATE CREAM

110g Organic whole milk
90g Organic cream
1 Mexico vanilla pod
Blanc Satin 29.2% (Cacao Barry), to taste
16g Organic butter

CHOCOLATE SPONGE CAKE

70g Organic whole milk
80g Organic sugar
175g Tanzanie 75% (Cacao Barry)
100g Butter
590g Pasteurised egg whites
260g Pasteurised egg yolks
180g Flour
60g Cocoa
1g Gourmet salt

PAPAYA JUICE

50g Papaya
40g Ugli fruit
50g Organic orange
30g Lime
50g Passionfruit

THE GOLDEN EGG

100g Papaya juice
2g Gelespesa
500g Water
25g Powdered vegetable gelling agent

WHITE CHOCOLATE BRAZIL NUTS

1.2kg Brazil nuts
300g Organic honey
300g Organic sugar
115g Blanc Satin 29.2% (Cacao Barry), melted
1g Mayan Sun gourmet sea salt

PROCESS

MAGNA CAKE

Parboil the whole milk together with the sugar and pour it over the chopped chocolate. Add the butter and then the egg whites and yolks. Sift the flour and cocoa and blend it together with the milk, sugar and chocolate. Add the salt. Cool until the mixture changes to a solid mass and then it is ready for serving. Gently place 25g on a plate for serving. Sprinkle some cocoa on the cake. Use a blow torch to heat without burning, until the thin crust becomes hard and the cake becomes soft and warm inside. Put a glass over the magna cake and fill it with smoke from the cocoa bean.

AVOCADO ICE CREAM

Combine the condensed milk, mineral water, sugar vanilla bean, cream and egg yolks and heat the mixture till the temperature is 72°C. Pour it over the chopped chocolate. Blend the avocado together with the lime juice and then blend it with the chocolate. Freeze the cream in a cup. When the ice cream is deep frozen place it in a Pacojet and blend it. Softly scoop it and arrange along the other elements.

WHITE CHOCOLATE CREAM

Heat the milk, cream and the vanilla pod until it boils. Add the white chocolate. At 30°C add the softened butter. Leave the chocolate cream to cool at -18°C for 2 hours. Whip it and spray small tops on a baking sheet by using an icing bag.

CHOCOLATE SPONGE CAKE

Heat the whole milk with the sugar and bring it to boiling point. Gently pour it over the chopped chocolate. Add the softened butter and then the eggs. Sift the flour and cocoa and then combine it with the mixture. Add the salt and blend everything together. Pour the dough into a siphon. Take a plastic cup with holes. Fill in the dough until two-thirds of the cup is full. Bake in the microwave oven on high for 55 seconds.

JUICE

Juice all the ingredients in a juicer.

THE GOLDEN EGG

Blend the juice and pour it into some half ball-shaped measuring cups of rubber sized 1.5 x 3cm and then freeze the juice. Heat the water and powdered vegetable gelling agent, stirring until it boils. Place the frozen juice on a skewer and dip it twice into the warm liquid, reserve.

WHITE CHOCOLATE BRAZIL NUTS

Chop the Brazil nuts and roast them with the honey and sugar. Then mix 100g of the roasted nuts with chocolate and salt, spread them out on a plate and leave to cool.

ASSEMBLY

Lay out the components as pictured.

ADVENTURE

ENTREMET, BY PALLE SØRENSEN MAKES 2 CAKES, EACH SERVES 8

INGREDIENTS

PASTRY CRUST 1

33.7g Organic butter
18.7g Saint-Domingue 70% (Cacao Barry)
12.5g Egg yolks
23.3g Brown sugar
15.9g Sugar
8g Flour
35g Brazil nuts
2.5g Cocoa
19g Whipped egg whites

TRUFFLE

380g Fresh organic cream
100g Invert sugar
180g Glucose
445g Madagascar 67%
80g Butter

PASTRY CRUST 2

22g Organic sugar
23g Brazil nut flour
7g Organic flour
5g Cocoa
17g Organic egg whites
6g Organic cream
44g Organic egg whites
22.5g Icing sugar
1.5g Dried egg whites
15g Caramelised Brazil nuts

AVOCADO FROMAGE

⅛ Vanilla pod
7.5g Glucose
14g Organic cream
0.6 leaves Isinglass
30g Avocado

12g Organic lemon juice
59g Gently whipped organic cream

BASIC CREAM FOR THE MOUSSE

170g Organic whole milk
170g Organic cream
35g Organic sugar
80g Organic yolks

AMBRA MOUSSE

1.5 leaves Isinglass
105g Basic cream
86g Ambra 3% (Cacao Barry)
20g Gianduja nut chocolate (Cacao Barry)
160g Organic whipped cream
20g Brazil nuts

MADAGASCAR MOUSSE

3.5 leaves Isinglass
350g Basic cream
186g Madagascar 67% (Callebaut)
463g Organic whipped cream

GLAZE FOR THE PASTRY

200g Whole milk
240g Sugar
60g Cocoa
5 leaves Isinglass
120g Madagascar 67% (Callebaut)
60g Gianduja nut chocolate (Cacao Barry)
19g Miroira
60g Water

PROCESS

PASTRY CRUST 1

Combine the butter and the Saint-Domingue 70% and melt the mixture. Add the egg yolks, the brown sugar and the sugar. Then add the sifted flour, chopped Brazil nuts and cocoa. Gently fold in the whipped egg whites. Bake the crust in an edge plate at 185-190°C for 16-18 minutes then leave to cool.

TRUFFLE

Mix the organic cream, invert sugar and glucose. Heat until the temperature is 100°C. Then add the chopped chocolate and make an emulsion with a hand blender. Add the softened butter when the temperature is 30°C.

PASTRY CRUST 2

Gently mix together the first six ingredients with a spatula. Whip the egg

whites with icing sugar and the dried whites. Gently fold this mixture into the rest of the dough. Sprinkle with the caramelised Brazil nuts. Bake the crust at 195°C for 9 minutes.

AVOCADO FROMAGE

Combine the vanilla, the glucose and the organic cream and heat the mixture until it boils. Add the isinglass and blend the avocado, the lemon juice and then combine it with the cream. Add the gently whipped organic cream to the mix and cool.

BASIC CREAM FOR THE MOUSSE

Mix all the ingredients and heat while stirring until the temperature is 72°C.

AMBRA MOUSSE

Add the isinglass to the warm basic cream. Then add the melted ambra and the gianduja. At 30-32°C gently fold in the whipped cream and then add the caramelised Brazil nuts.

MADAGASCAR MOUSSE

Add the isinglass to the warm basic cream, then add the dark chocolate. Heat until the mix reaches 30-32°C then gently fold in the whipped cream and remove from the heat and cool.

GLAZE

Heat the whole milk with the sugar till 105°C. Add the cocoa, isinglass, chocolate and gianduja and blend. Mix the Miroira and water and then gently add it to the mixture. Leave for 24 hours and then reheat it until 33-35°C. Cover the frozen cake.

ASSEMBLY

Cut to a rectangle shape of 22.8cm length and cover with truffle, then layer the second crust on top. Then add the avocado fromage cut into 1.8 x 1.8 x 22.8cm rectangles. Cover this with the Ambra mousse 3.5cm high. Coat all sides with the Madagascar mousse the height should be 6.1cm. Freeze this until firm then coat with glaze and decorate.

EASTERN EUROPE

A REGION THAT'S COMPRISED OF MANY DIFFERENT CULTURES, ETHNICITIES, LANGUAGES AND HISTORIES, EASTERN EUROPE IS MADE UP OF MANY COUNTRIES WITH THE MOST WIDELY RECOGNISED SUB-REGIONS INCLUDING EAST CENTRAL EUROPE, THE BALTICS, SOUTHEASTERN EUROPE/ BALKANS AND EASTERN EUROPE.

Poland is one of Eastern Europe's most underrated countries, with it's beautiful mountains ideal for skiing and hiking to it's hidden old towns of Krakow, Zamosc and Gdansk. The Polish capital of Warsaw has evolved into a café culture that has embraced new world cuisine however visitors will still encounter highlights of the past in its reconstructed old town.

Turkey, brimming with history, is a land of vast open spaces and mountain ranges that continue for miles. Turkey's landscape is dotted with battlegrounds, ruined castles and the palaces of great empires. Heading to Istanbul, visitors will experience some of the most vibrant bars with an upbeat atmosphere and the modern Ottoman cuisine are said to the tastiest in the world. It is true that a substantial amount of the biggest chocolate suppliers in the world have moved to Central and Eastern Europe and this trend appears to have boosted the local market. The supplier migration has given international brands a stronger presence in the region.

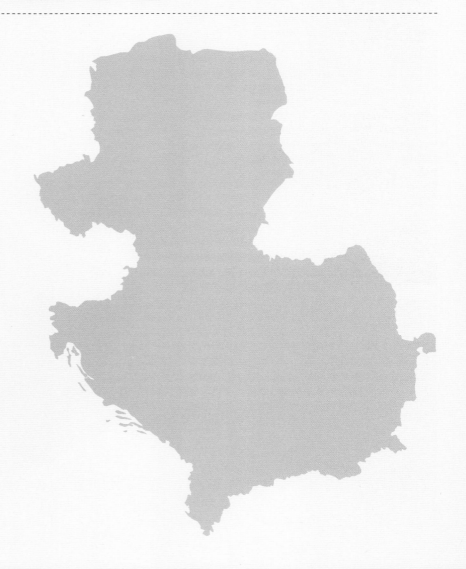

"IT IS TRUE THAT A SUBSTANTIAL AMOUNT OF THE BIGGEST CHOCOLATE SUPPLIERS IN THE WORLD HAVE MOVED TO CENTRAL AND EASTERN EUROPE."

WINNER

MARIUSZ BURRITA

EASTERN EUROPE

MARIUSZ BURRITA

Mariusz Buritta was born in Poland and has been working in the Sowa Patissierie in Poland since 1999. Now he is deputy manager in the decoration and pralines department. He has won many competitions including becoming the Polish champion in ice cream desserts, coming third in both the Culinary Olympics Erfurt and the Culinary World Cup Luxembourg. He is also champion of Polish confectioners.

SECOND PLACE

PETER DURAJ

Representing Slovakia at the Eastern Europe World Chocolate Master preselections Peter Ďuraj competed well for the place and was awarded with second prize overall. Peter has a great deal of experience with confectionary and works with chocolate at Alpha Chocolate DP confectionery, Slovakia.

THIRD PLACE

GAMZE BAS

Third prize at the Eastern Europe competition was awarded to Gamze Baş from Turkey who works at Lola's Luxury Chocolates confectionery in Ankara, Turkey. As well as the hope of improving her skills Gamze was also recognized at the competition for creating the best dipped praline.

JEWEL OF THE AZTECS
COATED PRALINE, BY MAURISZ BURRITA MAKES 50

INGREDIENTS

MARZIPAN WITH FRESH BASIL & MINT

150g Marzipan 'o'
10g Basil
5g Mint
10g French brandy

CRISPY MASS

100g Ginger cookies
125g Java Origine milk chocolate Callebaut
20g Cocoa butter
80g Pailleté Feuilletine Callebaut
250g Nut paste Callebaut PNP

LIME GANACHE

120g Cream 36%
36g Glucose syrup
280g Origine milk chocolate Java
80g Origine dark chocolate Mexico
24g Butter
80g Lime juice

Origine dark chocolate Mexico, to coat
Decoration of dark chocolate
Pieces of gold leaf

PROCESS

MARZIPAN WITH FRESH BASIL & MINT

Carefully knead the finely chopped basil and mint with the marzipan and brandy, and roll out between two sheets of acetate around 2-3mm thick.

CRISPY MASS

Break up the cookies. Melt the milk chocolate with the cocoa butter, and then combine with the rest of the ingredients.

LIME GANACHE

Bring the cream and glucose syrup to the boil, add the melted chocolates, soft butter and lime juice. Mix well. Create tiny decoration elements using small tube. Freeze them and sprayed with cocoa butter colorings for a velvety finishing.

ASSEMBLY

In a frame pour the crispy mass onto the marzipan layer, leave in a cool place to harden. Cut the filling using a guitar cutter into equal shapes and coat with dark tempered chocolate. Decorate with tiny lime ganache elements as well as chocolate decorative elements.

TEMPTATION OF QUETZALCOATL

MOULDED PRALINE, BY MARIUSZ BURRITA MAKES 50

INGREDIENTS

BLACKCURRANT GANACHE WITH VELVET WHITE CHOCOLATE

100g Granulated sugar
25g Glucose
125g Blackcurrant pulp
110g Cream 36%
200g White chocolate Callebaut Velvet
30g Cocoa butter
40g Butter

Barry glace, to coat
Or Noir chocolate, to coat
Dark chocolate Or Noir SOWA, to coat
Dark Crispearls Callebaut, to decorate
Silver decorative element, to decorate
Caramel decorative element, to decorate
Candied violet petals, to decorate

PROCESS

BLACKCURRANT GANACHE WITH VELVET WHITE CHOCOLATE

Caramelise the sugar, then add the glucose. Add the blackcurrant pulp and cream and bring to the boil. Cool down, then add the chocolate and butter.

ASSEMBLY

Spray the moulds with Barry glace then coat with moulds with dark Or Noir chocolate and leave to set. When firm fill with the blackcurrant ganache and set. When set close the moulds with dark chocolate and decorate.

INDIAN LAND TREASURE

ENTREMET, BY MAURISZ BURRITA SERVES 8

INGREDIENTS

CHOCOLATE SPONGE

6 Eggs
150g Granulated sugar
80g Dark chocolate Or Noir SOWA
30g Butter
80g Wheat flour
40g Potato flour
30g Cocoa powder Extra Brute Cacao Barry
4g Baking powder

VANILLA SYRUP

150g Water
150g Granulated sugar
5g Vanilla pod
45g Vanilla liqueur

RASPBERRY GANACHE

300g Cream 36%
95g Starch syrup
80g Raspberry pulp
210g Milk Origine chocolate Callebaut Java
225g Dark chocolate Callebaut Mexico
80g Butter
70g Vodka

CRISPY LAYER

120g Pailleté Feuilletine Callebaut
140g Milk chocolate Or Noir SOWA
60g Roasted almonds
160g Nut paste PNP Callebaut
50g Dark Crispearls Callebaut

CHOCOLATE MOUSSE

90g Egg yolks
60g Milk chocolate Or Noir SOWA
105g Dark chocolate Or Noir SOWA
6g Gelatine
15g Water
270g Cream 36%

PISTACHIO DACQUOISE WITH MATCHA TEA

150g Egg whites
100g Granulated sugar
100g Powdered sugar
80g Pistachios
15g Wheat flour
20g Matcha green tea

PASSIONFRUIT-MANGO MOUSSE

50g Egg yolks
50g Egg whites
15g Water
80g Granulated sugar
100g Mango pulp
70g Passionfruit pulp
12g Gelatine

CREME ANGLAISE

280g Milk 3.2%
80g Egg yolks
30g Granulated sugar

VANILLA MOUSSE WITH WHITE CHOCOLATE & NATURAL VANILLA

130g White chocolate Velvet Callebaut
160g Crème Anglaise
315g Cream 36%
10g Gelatine

9g Vanilla pod
40g Sugar syrup with exotic taste with 22 carat gold petals

RASPBERRY GEL

6g Gelatine
15g Water
210g Raspberry pulp
60g Fig pulp
60g Powdered sugar

SHINY GLAZE

400g Cream 36%
500g Granulated sugar
440g Water
100g Glucose syrup
200g Cocoa powder
70g Water
40g Gelatine

ASSEMBLY

Pieces of gold leaf

PROCESS

CHOCOLATE SPONGE

Beat the eggs with the sugar. Combine the melted chocolate with the melted butter. Mix together the wheat flour, potato flour, cocoa powder and baking powder and sift. Gently mix all the ingredients. Bake in a ring at 180°C for around 45 minutes.

VANILLA SYRUP

Mix all the ingredients but the liquor together and bring to the boil, cool and then add the liquor.

RASPBERRY GANACHE

Mix the cream and starch syrup then bring to the boil. Add the raspberry pulp and chocolates. Add the butter and vodka at the end.

CRISPY LAYER

Mix all the ingredients together.

CHOCOLATE MOUSSE

Beat the egg yolks, then add the melted chocolate and gelatine bloomed in the water. Stir gradually with the whipped cream. Mix well together.

PASSIONFRUIT-MANGO MOUSSE

Beat the egg yolks and egg whites, infuse with the water-sugar syrup, add the warm fruit pulps and dissolved gelatine.

PISTACHIO DACQUOISE WITH MATCHA TEA

Beat whites with sugar to stiff foam. Mix together the powdered sugar, chopped pistachios, flour and matcha tea then carefully add to the beaten egg whites. Bake in oven for 10 minutes at 180°C and then 10 minutes at 150°C.

CREME ANGLAISE

Bring the milk to the boil, add it to the beaten egg yolks and sugar. Mix well and put back on the heat and beat vigorously to obtain a temperature of 85°C.

VANILLA MOUSSE WITH WHITE CHOCOLATE & NATURAL VANILLA

Melt the chocolate in hot crème Anglaise at 40°C. Gradually combine with the whipped cream and gelatine, then add the vanilla pod and golden syrup.

RASPBERRY GEL

Dissolve the gelatine then mix with the rest of ingredients.

SHINY GLAZE

Bring the 440g water, cream, sugar and glucose syrup to the boil. Then add cocoa powder and gelatin soaked in 70g water. Bring to the boil, then mix and sieve.

ASSEMBLY

Soak the sponge with syrup. Cover it with the ganache and chill before adding the crispy layer ring and cover with chocolate mousse. Insert a layer of the frozen passionfruit-mousse into the centre of the cake and cover with pistachio dacquoise. Spread vanilla mousse over the top, add the raspberry gel. Freeze and coat with glaze.

FRANCE

THE MOST VISITED COUNTRY IN THE WORLD, FRANCE IS THE LAND OF CHIC, WHERE VISITORS CAN EXPERIENCE GOOD FOOD AND WINE, FAMOUS LANDMARKS AND SOME THAT FEW HAVE HEARD OF, AS WELL AS ART AND ROMANCE AND INCREDIBLE MOUNTAIN SCENERY.

The vibrant city of Paris is considered as one of the most beautiful cities on the earth and taking time to enjoy this wonderful city like a true Parisian is an unforgettable experience. Other hotspots include Nice, St-Tropez, Brittany, Normandy and not forgetting the Alps, a perfect location for skiing in the winter and hiking in the summer.

France was the second country in Europe where chocolate was introduced. Some outstanding chocolate products have emerged from France which are sold around the world as well as being the home of Barry Callebaut with their offices just outside of Paris. The idea of chocolate being used as an aphrodisiac flourished in the French courts and it seemed that art and literature was thick with erotic imagery inspired by chocolate. Using chocolate as a method of seduction was an idea that first emerged in France.

"SOME OUTSTANDING
CHOCOLATE PRODUCTS HAVE
EMERGED FROM FRANCE WHICH
ARE SOLD AROUND THE WORLD
AS WELL AS BEING THE HOME OF
BARRY CALLEBAUT."

WINNER

XAVIER BERGER

FRANCE

XAVIER BERGER

Xavier Berger is a graduate of a CAP Pâtissier Chocolatier Glacier Confiseur. He started in the chocolate factory Berger which was admitted in the Relais Dessert International in 2010. Xavier has taken part in many competitions and has won the Festival Occitanie, Les disciples d'Escoffier (Montpellier) and the La Cabosse d'Or (Lorient). Xavier enjoys learning new things and working in different establishments.

SECOND PLACE

SOPHIE LAUGEL

Sophie Laugel is currently head of pastry baking at Hochfelden Patisserie. She has trained in many areas including pastry, chocolate and technical trades as well as holding a Bachelor of Technology from catering school. Previously she has taken part in many competitions including Strasbourg chocolate fair where she came first and taking part in the French World Chocolate Master preselections where her showpiece won first place.

THIRD PLACE

PAUL CHAUVAUX

Competitions are second nature for pastry chef Paul Chauvaux, as he has been involved in many around France. As well as a winner of the Best French Apprentice in 2004 and receiving first prize at the Coupe de France Young Chocolatiers award in 2008, Paul has received third prize at the French World Chocolate Master preselection. Paul is trained in pastry and has a strong interest in chocolate.

MEXICO

COATED PRALINE, BY XAVIER BERGER MAKES 50

INGREDIENTS

MEXICO

60g Lime pulp (sweetened by 10%)
26g Invert sugar
15g Glucose DE60
26g Sorbitol powder
1.5g Lime zest
98g Extra Bitter Guyaquil
113g Lait Excellent 845
26g Cocoa butter
26g Anhydrous butter

Fleur de Cao, to coat

PROCESS

MEXICO

Melt together at 35°C the dark couverture, the milk couverture and the cocoa butter. Heat the lime pulp with the invert sugar syrup, the glucose and the sorbitol. Pour a third of this mixture over the melted couverture and beat the emulsion with a whisk. When the emulsion is ready, pour the remaining two-thirds over the couverture and mix with a hand blender. Add the lime zest and the anhydrous butter. Mix for a few seconds.

ASSEMBLY

When the ganache is at 32°C, pour into a tray with a height of 1cm. Allow to set. Spread a thin layer of chocolate over it and then cut into the desired shapes.

BRASILIA

MOULDED PRALINE, BY XAVIER BERGER MAKES 50

INGREDIENTS

BRASILIA

150g Caster sugar
100g Whipping cream 35%
25g Glucose DE60
125g Ganache couverture
150g Passionfruit pulp (sweetened to 10%)
8 drops Pink peppercorn extract

Dark chocolate 70.30.42, to coat

PROCESS

BRASILIA

Make a light caramel from the glucose
and the sugar. Gradually cool using with
the cream. Add the passionfruit pulp.
Pour over the couverture and mix. Add
the drops of pink peppercorn extract. Mix
for a few seconds.

ASSEMBLY

Coat the moulds with green stripes and
70.30.42. When the ganache is at 29°C, fill
the semi-spherical moulds and leave for 24
hours until set.

CALLAO

PLATED DESSERT, BY XAVIER BERGER SERVES 9

INGREDIENTS

CHOCOLATE FINANCIER

120g Almond paste 63%
60g Icing sugar
100g Yolk
50g Egg
1 Vanilla pod
47.5g Flour
47.5g Cocoa powder
47.5g Whipped egg white
60g Caster sugar
47.5g Melted butter

LIME MARMALADE

2 limes
½ apple
60g Granulated sugar
1.5 pinch Pectin NH

CHOCOLATE CREMEUX

112.5g Whipping cream
112.5g Milk
75g Yolk
70g Sugar
67.5g Mexique
67.5g Alto el Sol

LIME PARFAIT

127.5g Milk
60g Yolk
49.5g Caster sugar
37.5g Lime pulp (sweetened by 10%)
135g Whipped cream
8 drops Lime extract
1.5 sheets Gelatine
16.5g Water

CRISPY CHOCOLATE TUILE

200g Fondant
150g Glucose
125g Dark couverture 70%

GREEN APPLE JELLY

200g Green apple pulp (sweetened by 10%)
1 sheet Gelatine
11g Water

PROCESS

CHOCOLATE FINANCIER

Mix together the almond paste and the icing sugar. Gradually add the yolks and whites. Add the vanilla. Add the sifted flour and cocoa powder. Finally, add the cold melted butter. Pour into a flexiplan tray. Cook at 190°C for approximately 40 minutes.

LIME MARMALADE

Cut the apple into thin slices. Cut the limes into skinless sections. Heat and add the pectin mixture and sugar. Heat to the pearl stage. Remove from the heat and place to one side.

CHOCOLATE CREMEUX

Heat the milk, cream, yolks and sugar to 65°C. Pour over the couvertures and mix. Cool and place to one side.

LIME PARFAIT

Heat the milk, eggs and sugar using a bain-marie to 84°C. Add the melted gelatine. Cool using a whisk while adding the lime pulp and the extract. When the mixture is cool, add the whipped cream. Pour into the tubes. Store in the deep freeze at -20°C.

CRISPY CHOCOLATE TUILE

Heat the fondant and the glucose to 150°C. Add the melted couverture. Pour onto a Silpat to cool and then mix together. Using a stencil, create rectangles 3cm in width and 12.5cm in length. Bake at 160°C for 5 minutes. Remove from oven and store in an airtight container.

GREEN APPLE JELLY

Dissolve the gelatine and add the green apple. Mark into squares and place to one side.

ASSEMBLY

Place the chocolate financier in the centre of the plate. Use a bag to pipe an outline of chocolate cremeux around the top of the financier. Fill this outline with lime marmalade. Place the crispy chocolate tuile on top of this. Use a bag to add chocolate cremeux. Finally, put in place the lime parfait. Decorate and serve.

LIMA

ENTREMET, BY XAVIER BERGER MAKES 2 CAKES, EACH SERVES 8

INGREDIENTS

VANILLA SABLE

150g Butter
60g Caster sugar
6g Vanilla sugar
214g Pastry flour

CHOCOLATE DACQUOISE

180g Egg white
45g Caster sugar
180g Ground almonds
180g Caster sugar
18g Cornstarch
18g Cocoa powder
36g Crushed toasted almonds

ORANGE MARMALADE

200g Orange
100g Apple
320g Granulated sugar

BERGAMOT CHOCOLATE CREMEUX

88.5g Milk
88.5g Cream
60g Yolk
56g Sugar
22g Earl Grey tea
107g Mexique

ALTO ET SOL CHOCOLATE MOUSSE

180g Sugar
55.5g Water
120g Yolk
180g Egg
480g Alto el Sol
624g Whipped cream

DARK CHOCOLATE GLAZE

308g Sugar
80g Water
228g Cream
116g Glucose
86g Cocoa powder
36g Invert sugar syrup
16g Gelatine powder
72g Boiling water

PROCESS

VANILLA SABLE

Beat together the butter, caster sugar and vanilla sugar until pale. Add the sifted pastry flour. Roll out to 2mm thickness. Cut out the 18cm diameter bases. Bake at 180°C in an oven for 15 minutes.

CHOCOLATE DACQUOISE

Beat the whites with the caster sugar. Add the sifted almond and caster sugar mixture, cornstarch and cocoa powder together. Add the toasted almonds. Place into 18cm diameter tins. Bake at 190°C for 20 minutes.

ORANGE MARMALADE

Scrub and wash the oranges well. Cut into thin slices using a mandoline. Peel the apples and cut into thin slices. Mix with the sugar. Heat until the pearl stage.

BERGAMOT CHOCOLATE CREMEUX

The day before cooking infuse the tea in the cream and milk. On the following day strain the tea and increase the weight of the cream and milk to 177g using half milk and half cream. Heat the cream, milk, yolks and sugar to 70°C. Pour over the couverture and mix. Pour into the 18cm diameter rings. Store in the deep freeze at -20°C.

ALTO ET SOL CHOCOLATE MOUSSE

Heat the sugar and water to 121°C. Pour over the yolk and egg mixture. Beat and cool with a whisk. When the mixture is cool, add the Alto el Sol couverture to the cream. Add the base. Use immediately.

DARK CHOCOLATE GLAZE

Heat the water and sugar to 120°C. Heat to 60°C the cream, glucose, cocoa powder and invert sugar syrup. When the mixture is at 60°C, add the gelatine, mixed in advance with water. Use at approximately 40°C. Mix before use.

ASSEMBLY

Cover the base of a 20cm ring with the sable. Add the Alto el Sol mousse. Add the chocolate dacquoise. Place the insert with the orange marmalade on top of the dacquoise. Finish with the Alto el Sol mousse. Glaze. Decorate.

GERMANY

SITUATED IN CENTRAL EUROPE, GERMANY IS THE CONTINENT'S MOST POPULOUS COUNTRY AND HAS BECOME A POLITICAL AND CULTURAL HOTSPOT.

Few cities have seen as many changes over recent years as Berlin, the capital city, especially now that the two separate entities that existed before the Wall have come together as one. Berlin is renowned for its diverse culture so that tourists either find themselves in an elegant boulevard, or alternatively, in one of the city's more contemporary neighbourhoods. The city also plays host to various museums, green oasis' and nightlife galore.

Another popular city to visit is Munich which is known for reveling in it's own contradictions. Folklore and age-old traditions exist side-by-side with sleek BMWs, designer boutiques and signatures of a high-powered industry. However despite such sophistication, there is a touch of provincialism that remains and that many visitors find endearing. Its museums include world-class collections of artistic masterpieces, and there is a thriving music and culture scene in the city. Other exciting and vibrant cities to visit include Cologne, Dusseldorf and Hamburg, all with something slightly different to offer. The cuisine of each region varies greatly and a highlight is sampling the local dishes of each area whilst traveling through the country.

German chocolate can only be described as understated. World War Two left

companies like Stollwreck and Ritter Sport in a difficult situation, however despite this setback Germany has produced and continues to make, high quality chocolate that is sold and appreciated around the world.

"GERMANY HAS PRODUCED AND CONTINUES TO MAKE, HIGH QUALITY CHOCOLATE THAT IS SOLD AND APPRECIATED AROUND THE WORLD."

WINNER

JANA RISTAU
GERMANY

JANA RISTAU

By participating in the German Chocolate Masters the confectioner from Cologne wanted to challenge herself and to gather further experience in competitions. In an exciting contest she convinced the jury by her outstanding creations. Her chocolate showpiece was quite an inspiration showing an excellent interpretation of the contest theme and her technical skills. Further more Jana's dessert was described as delicious in taste and a great composition. Jana currently works at Törtchen Törtchen in Cologne.

SECOND PLACE

CAROLIN FAHRBACH

The master confectioner from Bad Friedrichshall is pastry chef at the confectioner Härdtner. She has been successful in several competitions. Her passion for working with chocolate as well as the wish to gain more experience in this field were the major reasons for her participation in the German Chocolate Masters.

THIRD PLACE

LISA RABE

The master confectioner from Rostock works in a chocolate manufacture in Rostock. She started her competition career at the German Chocolate Masters. She showed her expertise in technical skills as well as in her artistic showpiece.

THE EYE OF XIUHTECUHTLI

COATED PRALINE, BY JANA RISTAU MAKES 50

INGREDIENTS

PAPRIKA GELEE DE FRUITS

100g Paprika purée
38g Raspberry purée
63g Water
19g Sugar
6g Pectin NH
225g Sugar
63g Glucose
3.7g Neutral acid

TELLY CHERRY PEPPER GANACHE

85g Cream
40g Sorbitol
35g Invert sugar
4g Telly cherry pepper
75g Couverture 70%
175g Couverture 55%
50g Butter
5g Cocoa butter

PAPRIKA REDUCTION

100g Paprika juice

Dark chocolate, to coat

PROCESS

PAPRIKA GELEE DE FRUITS

Heat the purée over a low heat. Heat the water to 60°C then combine with the 19g of sugar and pectin. Blend the sugar/water solution with the fruit purée mix and bring to the boil. Slowly add the 225g sugar and glucose and bring to 109°C. Once it has reached 109°C start to cool and when no longer boiling stir in the neutral acid.

TELLY CHERRY PEPPER GANACHE

Bring the cream, sorbitol, sugars and pepper to boiling point and infuse for 10 minutes. Sieve in to the couvertures and blend until homogenous. Stir in the butters.

PAPRIKA REDUCTION

Reduce the paprika juice in a small sauteuse until it has the desired consistency.

ASSEMBLY

Pour the gelée into the frame immediately and leave to cool. Pour the ganache into the frame over the chilled gelée and leave to cool. When cool cover with a thin layer of dark chocolate, make a small dip at the top of the praline for the paprika reduction

AROMATIC DREAM

MOULDED PRALINE, BY JANA RISTAU MAKES 50

INGREDIENTS

GOAT'S MILK CARAMEL

60g Sugar
20g Glucose syrup
80g Goat's milk
20g Butter
60g Cacao Barry Ghana milk chocolate

MILK CHOCOLATE GANACHE

100g Cream
20g Sorbitol
20g Invert sugar (trimoline)
6g Telly cherry pepper
0.25g Cumin
0.25g Oregano
25g Butter
225g Cacao Barry Ghana milk chocolate

Cacao Barry Ghana milk chocolate, to coat

PROCESS

GOAT'S MILK CARAMEL

Caramelise the sugar and glucose over a low heat until golden brown. Deglaze with goat's milk and stir in the butter. Blend with the chocolate until the mix has blended.

MILK CHOCOLATE GANACHE

Bring the cream, sorbitol, sugars, herbs and spices to boiling point. Infuse for 10 minutes and sieve onto the chocolate. Mix until smooth and then blend in the butter.

ASSEMBLY

Temper chocolate and pour into the mould to have a thin shell. Once the caramel's temperature has reached 25°C pour into the moulds. Once the ganache is at 25°C pour on top of the caramel. Pour a think layer of chocolate on top of the ganache to seal the moulds. When set take them out of the moulds and decorate.

THE TRANSFORMATION OF COCOA BY CHANTICO (GODDESS OF THE HEARTH)

PLATED DESSERT, BY JANA RISTAU SERVES 6

INGREDIENTS

CARAMEL SAUCE

200g Sugar
100g Cream
1.5g Salt
125g Butter

SPICED BROWNIE

49g Venezuela couverture
0.3g Chilli powder
1.2g Cinnamon powder
65g Whole egg
98g Sugar
77g Butter
53g Flour
32g Pecan nuts, roasted and chopped

SAPODILLA SORBET

325g Water
125g Sugar
500g Sapodilla purée
50g Dextrose
50g Tamarind purée

CHOCOLATE MOUSSE

45g Egg yolk
25g Sugar
½ sheet Gelatine
75g Couverture 70%
150g Cream

CARAMEL CREME FILLING

90g Sugar
310g Cream
100g Milk
25g Sugar
40g Egg yolk
2g Salt
3½ sheets Gelatine, bloomed

CHOCOLATE GELEE

2 sheets gelatine
115g Water
275g Milk chocolate

CARAMELISED AMARANTH SEED

30g Sugar
10g Amaranth seed, popped

CARAMEL 'KNIFE' SHAPE

120g Glucose syrup
15g Butter
180g Fondant
40g Almond flakes, roasted

CARAMEL 'WATERING' TROUGH

100g Sugar
200g Water
1.5g Cinnamon powder

PROCESS

CARAMEL SAUCE

Caramelise the sugar to desired colour and deglaze with the heated cream. Add the salt and bring to 105°C boil. Mix in the butter and cool completely, cover.

SPICED BROWNIE

Melt the couverture, spices and butter together. Combine the whole egg with sugar and stir into the chocolate mixture. Blend together the flour and nuts, stir into mixture, place mixture in the appropriate mould and bake at 180°C.

SAPODILLA SORBET

Heat the water and sugars until the sugar is completely dissolved. Mix in the remaining ingredients and pour into two Pacojet beakers. Freeze completely and purée in frozen state with Pacojet as required.

CHOCOLATE MOUSSE

Whip up egg yolk until it increases in volume. Heat the sugar to 118°C and combine with egg yolk and whip. Melt the gelatine and also add to the egg yolk. Melt the couverture at 50°C; stir in one-third of the cream; fold in the egg yolk mixture and then fold in the rest of the cream.

CARAMEL CREME FILLING

Caramelise the sugar until dark and deglaze with the cream and milk. Mix sugar and egg yolk and combine with the hot liquid. Mix in salt and gelatine and blend until smooth.

CHOCOLATE GELEE

Heat the gelatine in water and blend with milk chocolate couverture until homogenous.

CARAMELISED AMARANTH SEED

Caramelise the sugar, add the amaranth seed and continue to cook until brown.

CARAMEL 'KNIFE' SHAPE

Combine the glucose syrup and butter, bring to boil and continue boiling at 154°C. Stir in warm almond flakes and pour onto a silpat mat. Allow to cool completely; break into pieces, mix and sprinkle in the desired form and melt in the oven.

CARAMEL 'WATERING' TROUGH

Caramelise the sugar until dark and deglaze with the water. Boil caramel until easily comes away from sides of pot, add cinnamon and leave to cool fully.

ASSEMBLY

Decorate the plate with a brushstroke of caramel sauce. Put the spiced brownie at one side. Add one scoop of sapodilla sorbet and one of chocolate mousse on top of the brownie. Place the chocolate gelée on a foil. Add a thick layer of caramel crème on top and roll up and chill. When cold remove the foil, cut it into equal pieces and arrange it on the plate. Decorate with salt and caramelised amaranth seed. Decorate the mousse with the caramel shapes.

SWEET GOLD OF CENTEOTL (GOD OF CORN)

ENTREMET, BY JANA RISTAU MAKES 2 CAKES, EACH SERVES 8

INGREDIENTS

ALMOND CRUMBLE

115g Butter
75g Sugar
150g Flour
115g Ground almonds
1g Baking powder
Salt, to taste

MANGO GELEE

25g Passionfruit purée
225g Mango purée
5g Gelatine
25g Sugar
0.5g Xanthan gum

CREME DE MANGO

170g Mango purée
15g Passionfruit purée
5.5g Gelatine
85g Milk
60g Cream, beaten until creamy not stiff
25g Sugar

POPCORN DECOCTION

25g Canola oil
100g Popcorn
7g Sea salt
90g Butter
75g Sugar
750g Milk

MILK CHOCOLATE POPCORN MOUSSE

180g Popcorn decoction
10g Sugar
1½ sheets Gelatine
12g Egg yolk
230g 'Ghana' couverture
255g Cream, beaten until creamy not stiff

CARAMELISED POPCORN

25g Popcorn
75g Sugar

DARK CHOCOLATE MOUSSE

180g Egg yolk
100g Sugar
2 sheets Gelatine
300g Couverture 70%
600g Cream, beaten until creamy not stiff

CHOCOLATE COATING

200g Cream
280g Water
360g Sugar
300g Glucose
60g Cocoa powder
600g 'Venezuela' couverture
50g Cocoa butter
80g Dark rum, brown

PROCESS

ALMOND CRUMBLE

Combine all ingredients to make streusel. Bake at 150-160°C until golden brown.

MANGO GELÉÉ

Heat the purées and dissolve gelatine in the purée mixture. Combine sugar with xanthan gum, blend and add on top of the crumble.

CREME DE MANGO

Heat the purées and dissolve gelatine in the purée mixture. Stir in the milk. Fold in cream and sugar at 30°C and add to torte creation.

POPCORN DECOCTION

Combine all ingredients and bring to boil. Blend well and leave to infuse for as long as possible. Sieve.

MILK CHOCOLATE POPCORN MOUSSE

Heat the decoction with sugar and gelatine to 80-85°C, add egg yolk. Add the couverture and blend until homogenous. Fold in the cream at 45°C.

CARAMELISED POPCORN

Caramelise the popcorn in the sugar until golden brown.

DARK CHOCOLATE MOUSSE

Beat egg yolk until increases in volume, heat sugar to 118°C and combine with egg yolk. Dissolve gelatine and add, melt the couverture at 55°C; stir in one-third of the cream. Fold in the egg yolk mixture and fold in the rest of the cream.

CHOCOLATE COATING

Combine together the cream, water, sugar and glucose and cocoa and bring to boil. Add the couverture and cocoa butter, mix and then add the rum. Leave to cool overnight.

ASSEMBLY

In a 16cm round tin make a lyer of streusel and chill. When set add a layer of mango gelée, then add a layer of popcorn chocolate mousse mixed with popcorn and chill. then add a thin layer of mango cream and freeze. When frozen remove from the tin and place in a 18cm cake tin. Fill the sides with the dark chocolate mousse, smooth and freeze. Finally remove from the mould and coat with chocolate coating warmed to 30°C.

ICELAND

OFTEN REFERRED TO AS THE LAND OF 'ICE AND FIRE', ICELAND IS COMPRISED OF VOLCANIC ERUPTIONS, BEAUTIFUL GLACIERS AND WATERFALLS. AN INSPIRATION TO ARTISTS AND PHOTOGRAPHERS, ICELAND HAS LANDSCAPES LIKE NO OTHER.

The capital city, Reykjavik, is made up of more than half of Iceland's population and is in an area of geothermal hot springs which for the people of Iceland creates a natural central heating system and pollution-free environment. For a capital city, Reykjavik is relatively small but has built up a reputation for partying and therefore the city has a fun and vibrant atmosphere.

During the winter, Iceland is renowned for its green, blue, yellow and pink lights of the aurora in the night sky which are something of a delight. To fully embrace the unique Icelandic culture it is essential for visitors to bathe in turquoise pools, come face-to-face with a whale and visit the stunning mountains. When it comes to Icelandic cuisine modern Icelandic bakeries offer a wide selection of breads and pastry. Local favourites include snuour, a type of cinnamon roll topped with glaze or melted chocolate and skuffukaka, a single layer chocolate cake baked in a roasting pan, covered with chocolate glaze and sprinkled with ground coconut.

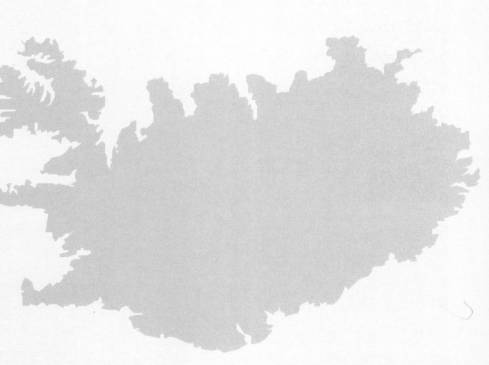

"WHEN IT COMES TO ICELANDIC CUISINE MODERN ICELANDIC BAKERIES OFFER A WIDE SELECTION OF BREADS AND PASTRY."

WINNER

ASGEIR SANDHOLT

ICELAND

ASGEIR SANDHOLT

First place in the Scandinavia preselection went to Asgeir Sandholt from Iceland. From 1996 to 2000 Asgeir was pastry chef at Lars Hjort Konditori in EUC Ringsted, Copenhagen. Later in 2000 he started the Sandholt Bakery in Reykjavik, Iceland. Asgeir has won a number of awards and competitions in Denmark and Iceland, and is very happy to be in the final in Paris and to get a chance to learn more about the Chocolate World!

CACTUS GINGER GIANDUJA

COATED PRALINE, BY ASGEIR SANDHOLT MAKES 240

INGREDIENTS

CACTUS FRUIT PASTE

330g Citrus fruit cocktail purée
25g Fresh ginger juice
33g Sugar
7g Apple pectin
300g Sugar
68g Glucose
8g Citric acid

GINGER GANACHE

230g Cream 36%
75g Invert sugar
3g Lemon zest
600g Lactée Supérieure 38%
60g Ginger juice
120g Butter

CRISPY GIANDUJA

450g Gianduja
350g Crispy French nougat

CRISPY FRENCH NOUGAT

70g Lavender honey
10g Glucose
145g Sugar
20g Glucose
30g Egg whites
10g Sugar
100g Almonds

Milk chocolate, to coat

PROCESS

CACTUS FRUIT PASTE

Bring the purée and ginger juice to the boil. Slowly add the 33g of sugar mixed with the pectin and stir. In three more steps add the remaining sugar and glucose. Boil to 105°C, add the citric acid and pour into a frame.

GINGER GANACHE

Heat the cream together with the invert sugar and lemon zest. Remove the lemon zest and emulsify the liquid with the chocolate. At 38°C add the ginger juice and butter. Mix well with an electric mixer and pour into the frame with the fruit paste. Leave to crystallise for 48-72 hours.

CRISPY GIANDUJA

Melt the gianduja and temper. Add the French nougat and pour into the frame with the previous two fillings so that the fruit paste is in the middle. Leave to crystallise.

CRISPY FRENCH NOUGAT

Cook the honey and 10g of glucose to 120°C. Separately heat the 145g sugar with the 20g glucose to 160°C. Slightly whip the egg whites together with the 10g sugar. Add the first mixture followed by the second one and mix together well. Finally incorporate the almonds, fill the nougat into an other frame and leave to rest. Once the nougat has cooled down, mix in a blender to obtain small pieces and add to the gianduja.

ASSEMBLY

Pure the gianduja in the same frame as the other two fillings and leave to crystallize. Cut the filling into the wished shape and cover with milk chocolate.

WALNUT TOFFEE COCOA BEAN

MOULDED PRALINE, BY ASGEIR SANDHOLT MAKES 150

INGREDIENTS

SPICY CHOCOLATE CARAMEL

180g Sugar
300g Cream 36%
120g Glucose
1 Mexican vanilla pod
0.2g Cinnamon
0.1g Nutmeg
20g Milk chocolate standard
20g Dark chocolate standard
1.5g Sea salt
75g Butter

WALNUT NOUGATINE

150g Icing sugar
2.5g NH pectin
125g Butter
50g Glucose
180g Walnuts

Dark chocolate, to coat

PROCESS

SPICY CHOCOLATE CARAMEL

Cook the sugar until you obtain a dark caramel. Deglaze with the cream and glucose, previously mixed. Add the spices and cook at 106°C. Allow the caramel to cool down, then emulsify with the chocolates. At 35°C add the butter and the sea salt, mix well with an electric mixer.

WALNUT NOUGATINE

Combine the sugar and the pectin, followed by the butter and glucose. Heat everything slowly until you obtain a smooth texture. Add the crushed walnuts, spread on a silicone sheet and bake at 190°C.

ASSEMBLY

Brush bronze and white cocoa butter into the cocoa bean moulds followed by dark chocolate. Fill the obtained shells halfway with the caramel, and then add the walnut nougatine. Finally close with dark chocolate and leave to set.

FRUITY XOCOLATL

PLATED DESSERT, BY ASGEIR SANDHOLT SERVES 10

INGREDIENTS

GUAVA MANGO SAUCE

15g Fresh lime juice
60g Fresh guava
60g Fresh mango
Zest of 1 lime
150g Mango purée
150g Guava purée

LIME JELLY

70g Neutral glaze
15g Acacia honey
35g Fresh lime juice
2g Lime zest

GINGER TOFFEE

125g Sugar
45g Clarified butter
240g Cream 36%
15g Glucose
20g Fresh ginger juice
165g Lactée Supérieure 38%

COCOA NIBS ICE CREAM

125g Sugar
4g Stabiliser
560g Milk 3, 6%
40g Non-fat milk powder
11g Invert sugar
40g Powdered glucose
115g Cocoa nibs
30g Egg yolks
205g Cream 36%

COCOA NIBS CRUMBLE

50g Cane sugar
50g Flour
50g Butter
25g Almond powder
25g Cocoa nibs, finely grated
5g Rose pepper
60g White chocolate standard
20g Cocoa butter

HOT CHOCOLATE MOUSSE

270g Milk
50g Sugar
1g Agar agar
60g Madagascar 64%

PROCESS

GUAVA MANGO SAUCE

Cut the fruits in small cubes and mix together with the lime zest and purées.

LIME JELLY

Combine all the ingredients and blend with a hand mixer.

GINGER TOFFEE

Caramelise the sugar. Deglaze the caramel with the clarified butter followed by the cream mixed with the glucose and ginger juice. Slowly add this mixture to the melted chocolate. Emulsify and leave to crystallise overnight.

COCOA NIBS ICE CREAM

Mix half of the sugar with the stabiliser. Heat the milk together with the milk powder and glucose. Add the sugar followed by the cocoa nibs, previously heated. Finally add the sugar/stabiliser mix and the egg yolks previously mixed with the cream. Heat to 85°C and leave to rest overnight.

COCOA NIBS CRUMBLE

Lightly mix together the sugar, flour, butter, almond powder and cocoa nibs and bake at 150°C. Leave the crumble to cool before blending it together with the white chocolate, cocoa butter and rose pepper. Place in a silicone mould and leave to set.

HOT CHOCOLATE MOUSSE

Heat the milk. Add the sugar together with the agar agar and bring to the boil. Emulsify with the chocolate and keep this mixture in a siphon at about 45°C. Serve á la minute.

ASSEMBLY

Take the crumble out of the silicone mould and place in the centre of the disc. Pipe the ginger toffee around half of the crumble and place the guava-mango pieces on it followed by the sauce and lime jelly. The ice cream is placed on the crumble and the hot chocolate mousse squeezed on the other side right before serving.

EXOTIC LABYRINTH

ENTREMET, BY ASGEIR SANDHOLT MAKES 2 CAKES, EACH SERVES 8

INGREDIENTS

CHOCOLATE SPONGE

100g Eggs
30g Invert sugar
50g Sugar
30g Almond powder
50g Flour
3g Baking powder
10g Cocoa powder
32g Butter
50g Cream
20g Dark chocolate standard

EXOTIC CRUMBLE

25g Freeze-dried pineapple
130g Almond crumble
30g Organic coconut flakes
35g Gold flakes
1g Salt
10g Cane sugar
½ Mexican vanilla pod
120g White chocolate

ALMOND CRUMBLE

35g Butter
35g Sugar
35g Flour
35g Almond powder

CITRUS TOFFEE

220g Sugar
80g Clarified butter
250g Cream 36%
10g Orange zest
310g Lactée Caramel 31%
125g Fresh lemon juice
30g Glucose

WHITE CHOCOLATE MOUSSE WITH COCONUT

7g Gelatine
175g Coconut purée
1 Mexican vanilla pod
220g White chocolate
20g Cocoa butter
345g Whipped cream

MADAGASCAR CHOCOLATE MOUSSE

4g Gelatine
250g Milk
305g Madagascar 64%
500g Whipped cream

PINEAPPLE CUBES

175g Pineapple
Zest from 1 lemon
Zest from 1 lime

EXOTIC CREAM

3g Gelatine
200g Passionfruit purée
100g Pineapple purée
50g Coconut purée
200g Egg yolks
225 Whole eggs
210g Sugar
240g Butter

WHITE CHOCOLATE SPRAY

100g Cocoa butter
230g White chocolate standard

PROCESS

CHOCOLATE SPONGE

Mix the eggs with the invert sugar and sugar. Add the almond powder, flour, baking powder and cocoa powder. Melt the butter together with the cream at 45°C and add to the previous mixture. Finally add the chocolate melted at 45°C. Leave the dough to rest overnight. Bake at 180°C.

EXOTIC CRUMBLE

Mix all the dry ingredients together followed by the melted chocolate.

ALMOND CRUMBLE

Lightly mix all the ingredients together and bake at 160°C.

CITRUS TOFFEE

Cook the sugar to the caramel stage. Stir in the clarified butter and deglaze with the

mixture of cream, glucose and orange zest. Emulsify with the chocolate and finally add the lemon juice. Leave to crystallise.

WHITE CHOCOLATE MOUSSE WITH COCONUT

Soak the gelatine in cold water. Bring the coconut purée together with the vanilla to the boil, add the drained gelatine and emulsify with the white chocolate and cocoa butter previously melted. At 38°C add the lightly whipped cream.

MADAGASCAR CHOCOLATE MOUSSE

Soak the gelatine in cold water. Bring the milk to the boil, add the drained gelatine and emulsify with the chocolate. At 40°C add the lightly whipped cream.

PINEAPPLE CUBES

Cut the pineapple into cubes. Mix together with the zests and plastic wrap. Bake everything at 120°C for about 12 minutes to reduce the water.

EXOTIC CREAM

Soak the gelatine in cold water. Mix all the ingredients, except the butter, in a pan and bring to the boil. Add the drained gelatine. At 35°C mix in the butter with a blender. Leave to crystallise.

WHITE CHOCOLATE SPRAY

Melt the cocoa butter together with the chocolate.

ASSEMBLY

Once the sponge is baked, cut out two rings 14cm diameter. Take one of the two sponges and place it in a cake ring 14cm diameter. Spread some of the crumbles on top followed by drops of citrus toffee. Pour over the dark chocolate mousse and lay the second sponge on top. Finally pipe the exotic cream combined with the pineapple cubes on the sponge and freeze. Place the cake middle in the centre of a cake ring 16.5cm diameter. Close the cake with the white chocolate mousse and freeze. For finishing spray with white chocolate spray.

ITALY

A BEAUTIFUL COUNTRY, WHICH OFFERS EVERYTHING FROM A STUNNING AND VARIED COUNTRYSIDE TO AN ELABORATE SENSE OF FASHION, FEATURING THE MOST WONDERFUL CUISINE TO IT'S ARTISTIC LAURELS, ITALY HAS IT ALL.

With 44 sites, Italy has more UNESCO World Heritage sites than any other country on earth. With cities like Milan, Rome, Venice and Florence, it is no wonder that visitors flock to Italy in their thousands.

The frenetic, restless rhythm of Milan, known for being one step ahead, makes it difficult for visitors to not stay unmoved by all the cultural and social stimulus. A city full of contradictions, Milan features the ancient and modern, trends and counter-trends, fashion and underground, middle class and working class. Venice is possibly the city that has, in appearance, changed least throughout the decades and still remains stunning and completely unique. It plays host to many interesting towns; Burano, Murano, Padua and Vicenza to name a few. Other highlights include skiing in the Alps, hiking the Domomites or relaxing on Sardinia's golden coast.

But even when visiting all the sights, a trip to Italy would not be complete without fully embracing the Italian way of life, visitors must take the opportunity to enjoy a coffee at a streetside cafe or linger over a long lunch in the hot Mediterranean sun.

For those devoted to chocolate a trip to Italy is essential. An Italian classic is Gianduja, a confectionary that's now exported all over the world. Created in 1856 by Caffarel, Turin's oldest chocolatier, Gianduja is a paste of hazelnut and chocolate and is most commonly shaped as a triangle. Other Italian specialities include the Alpino (liquer-filled chocolates), Baci kisses (Barbero's dark chocolate studded with hazelnuts), and Gelato al Gianduja (Gianduja ice cream).

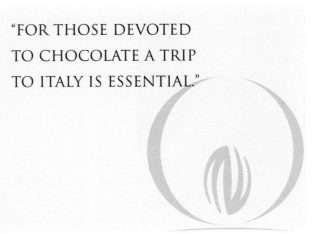

"FOR THOSE DEVOTED
TO CHOCOLATE A TRIP
TO ITALY IS ESSENTIAL."

WINNER

YUMIKO SAIMURA
ITALY

YUMIKO SAIMURA

Born in Kyoto, Japan, Yumiko arrived in Italy in 2004, where she attended high professional courses at the Institute Mellerio Rosmini in Domodossola. She has worked as a pastry chef for several Michelin-starred restaurants as Piccolo Lago and several renowned pastry shops such as Casa del Dolce Intra. The most important turning point in her career starts with the opening of her own pastry shop Piccola Pasticceria in Casale Monferrato in 2008. She has attended numerous professional training courses to develop her knowledge about the wide culture of cocoa and chocolate.

SECOND PLACE

FRANCESCO BOCCIA

For Francesco Boccia the most memorable part of the competition was getting to compete with the best chocolatiers and pastry chefs in Italy. Since 2003 Francesco has worked in the pastry shop owned by his parents although he has a lot of experience in confectionary having interned at the Gothenburg, Sweden and taken place in many competitions. Francesco is currently enrolled at the University of Naples studying a degree in food technology.

THIRD PLACE

SANDY ASTRALI

Sandy Astrali was awarded third place by the judges for the World Chocolate Masters Italian Preselection. At present Sandy is a pastry chef at Pasticceria Aurora di Tombolo (PD) and she has previously worked for restaurants and hotels. This chef has interned in China and taken part in many competitions including a runner-up in the Pastry Grand Prix held in Bucharest and winner of the best dessert at the Italian preselections. Sandy is from Tombolo and hopes to continue improving her chocolate skills in the future.

ENCOUNTER

COATED PRALINE, BY YUMIKO SAIMURA MAKES 100

INGREDIENTS

CITRUS GANACHE

200g Fresh cream 35%
1 Vanilla pod
Zest of 1 lemon
Zest of 1 orange
30g Glucose 42DE
30g Trimoline
40g Butter cream
20g Lemon juice
20g Orange juice
175g Chocolate Sao Thomè 70%
95g Milk Chocolate 2865 NV

PRALINE CREAM

225g Caramel coated Piedmont Hazelnuts
60g Mycryo

Dark Chocolate 5835 NV, to coat

PROCESS

CITRUS GANACHE

Boil the cream with the vanilla pod, lemon zest and orange zest, leave to infuse for an hour, then stain through a fine mesh sieve. Heat the mixture to 40°C and pour the glucose and Trimoline on to the chocolates melted to 45°C, blend with a hand blender for 1 minute.

Add the butter cream, lemon and orange enfused cream the lemon and orange juice, keep blending the mixture and then cool to room temperature, until it reaches a temperature of 31-32°C and stirring occasionally to keep a constant temperature.

PRALINE CREAM

In a container place the caramel coated Piedmont hazelnuts and melted Mycryo at 45°C. Use a spoon to mix the two ingredients and temper on marble at 22°C.

ASSEMBLY

Make a base of dark chocolate 5835 NV has to be poured into the mould after being hand-temperated. When cool add a layer of praline cream. Spread the citrus ganache on top of the praline cream and allow to crystallise for 24 hours at 15-18°C. Cut the chocolate and coat it with Dark Chocolate 5835 NV.

TREASURE

MOULDED PRALINE, BY YUMIKO SAIMURA MAKES 50

INGREDIENTS

PISTACHIO CREAM

13g White Velvet chocolate
75g Bronte pistachio paste
1 Vanilla pod

STRAWBERRY & LIME GELATINE

240g Strawberries, crushed
Zest of 1 lime
35g White cane sugar
52g Glucose 42DE
3g Pectin

ECUADOR GANACHE

125g Fresh cream 35%
3g Cardamom pods
20g Glucose 42DE
20g Trimoline
156g Ecuador chocolate 70%
43g Butter cream

Milk chocolate 2865 NV, to coat

PROCESS

PISTACHIO CREAM

In a container place the white chocolate melted at 45°C, the pistachio paste and the crushed vanilla pod. Using a spoon, mix the ingredients on marble and temper to 22°C. Pour into a piping bag and use.

STRAWBERRY & LIME GELATINE

Put the crushed strawberries in a pot with the lime zest and glucose, heat at 50°C and add the pectin and sugar mixed in advance. Cook at 103°C, cool in a blast freezer; pour into a piping bag and use.

ECUADOR GANACHE

Boil the cream with crumbled cardamom, leave to infuse for 15 minutes, strain through a fine mesh sieve. Heat the mixture to 40°C and pour the glucose and Trimoline onto the melted chocolate at 45°C, emulsify with a hand blender for one minute. Add the butter cream and continue blending for another minute, pour into a container, cool to temperature of 31-32°C, stirring occasionally to keep a uniform temperature. Pour into a piping bag and use.

ASSEMBLY

Coat the moulds with Milk chocolate 2865 NV and cool. First pipe in the Ecuador ganache and leave to set, then add the strawberry and lime gelatine and cool, finally a layer of pistachio cream and seal with more Milk chocolate 2865 NV.

FRESHNESS

PLATED DESSERT, BY YUMIKO SAIMURA SERVES 6

INGREDIENTS

CHOCOLATE CAKE

70g Butter, softened
55g Powdered sugar
65g Plain chocolate NV 58 35 56.3%
60g Egg yolks
1 Vanilla bean
120g Egg whites
55g White cane sugar
70g Plain biscuit flour

EXOTIC CREAM

45g Passionfruit, crushed
20g Mango, crushed
20g Coconut flesh
1 Vanilla bean
25g Egg yolks
20g White cane sugar
2g Gelatine
35g Butter

BAVARIAN WHITE CHOCOLATE

125g Crème Anglaise
75g Velvet White chocolate
4g Gelatine
150g Fresh cream 35%

PINEAPPLE ASPIC

50g Fresh pineapple, diced
Zest of 1/2 lime
75g Vanilla syrup
0.5g Agar agar

DARK ALMOND CRISP

50g Almond praline
20g Dark chocolate 5835NV 56.3%
15g Paillete Feuilletine

CHOCOLATE & MANGO MOUSSE

80g Crushed mango
2.5g Gelatine
25g Glucose 42DE
120g Arriba milk coating 39%
100g Fresh cream 35%

COCOA GLAZE

275g Water
250g Fresh cream 35%
125g Cocoa powder
275g White cane sugar
125g Glucose 42 DE
20g Gelatine

MANGO BALLS SAUTEED IN VANILLA

100g Mango, crushed
100g Syrup
1 Vanilla pod bourbon
10 Fresh mango balls

VANILLA SYRUP

350g Water
150g White cane sugar
2 Vanilla beans

PROCESS

CHOCOLATE CAKE

In a planetary mixer with a fine mesh whisk, whisk the soft but not melted butter, powdered sugar, Plain chocolate NV 58 35 56.3% melted at 40°C, the egg yolks and rushed vanilla bean. Separately whip the egg whites with sugar. Combine the two whipped mixtures using a marisa, add the sifted flour, being careful not to collapse the dough. Spread to 3mm. Bake for 10 minutes at 180°C. Cool down and cut with a smooth pastry ring with a diameter of 4.5cm.

EXOTIC CREAM

Heat the two crushed fruits, the coconut flesh and vanilla bean to 50°C. Mix the yolks and sugar with a whisk, incorporate the hot pulp in three parts. Continue to cook stirring until the cream has thickened (at 82°C). Allow to cool to 45°C, add the softened gelatine, butter and blend with a hand blender for 1 minute.

BAVARIAN WHITE CHOCOLATE

Pour the boiling crème Anglaise onto the chocolate pieces and the softened gelatine. Emulsify with a blender for a minute, allow the mixture to cool for 35°C. Add the cream, whipped.

PINEAPPLE ASPIC

Cut the pineapple into small cubes, add grated lime zest and stir with a spoon. Place vanilla syrup into a saucepan with the agar-agar and bring to a boil. Pour hot onto the pineapple mixture and use.

DARK ALMOND CRISP

Place the praline and the dark chocolate melted at 45°C in a container. Using a spoon mix the two ingredients and add the Paillete Feuilletine stirring constantly. Spread to a thickness of 3mm. Crystallise in a refrigerator and cut with a smooth pastry ring with a diameter of 4.5cm.

CHOCOLATE & MANGO MOUSSE

Heat the mango pulp to 60°C. Pour over gelatine and melted chocolate at 45°C for 2 minutes and emulsify with a hand blender. Cool to 35°C, add the cream, whipped with a fine mesh whip, then with a spatula.

COCOA GLAZE

Heat the water, cream and sugar. Separately mix the cocoa and sugar, add the cream mixture and cook at 104°C, stirring constantly. Incorporate the softened gelatine and blend at medium speed. Use when the mixture reaches 32°C.

MANGO BALLS SAUTEED IN VANILLA

Put the crushed mango in a pan with the syrup and vanilla. Reduce on a high heat at 100°C just for 1 minute. Add the fresh mango balls and continue cooking for 1 minute and cool, soak in vanilla syrup.

VANILLA SYRUP

Place all the ingredients in a saucepan and boil them until 60°C for 1 minute. Filter and let cool.

ASSEMBLY

With two cylindrical moulds one bigger than the other fill the small mould with a layer of chocolate cake and then half-full with exotic cream and place in a blast freezer. Pour Bavarian white chocolate into a silicone cylindrical mould filling up to 3mm from the rim. Pour pineapple aspic onto the Bavarian white chocolate to the rim of the mould and finish freezing. When frozen place remove from the smaller mould and place the small cylinder in the larger cylinder mould on a bed of the almond crisp. Fill with chocolate and mango mousse over the top and freeze. Unmould and frost with Cocoa Glaze at 32°C. Garnish with mango balls and a disc of chocolate.

BITTER SWEET MEXICO

ENTREMET, BY YUMIKO SAIMURA MAKES 2 CAKES, EACH SERVES 8

INGREDIENTS

SPONGE CAKE WITH PISTACHIO

200g Egg yolks
100g Granulated sugar
300g Egg whites
150g Granulated sugar
200g Biscuit flour
50g Starch
80g Bronte Pistachio paste

GRAND MARNIER BATH

250g Water
100g White cane sugar
1 Orange peel
2 Vanilla beans
30g Grand Marnier

CREME ANGLAISE
WITH VANILLA BOURBON

45g Fresh milk
1 Vanilla pod bourbon
150 Egg yolks
11 White cane sugar

MILK CHOCOLATE CREAM

170g Crème Anglaise
100g Milk Chocolate Java 32%
25g Hazelnut paste
2.5g Gelatine

RASPBERRY AND
STRAWBERRY GELATINE

85g Raspberries, crushed
55g Strawberries, crushed
2g Lime peel
25g Acacia honey
3.5g Gelatine

BAVARIAN MASCARPONE

40g Egg yolks
30g White can sugar
12g Dextrose
5g Gelatine
10g Espresso
250g Mascarpone
50g Fresh cream 35%
1 Vanilla bean Bourbon

HAZELNUT CRISP

200g Caramel coated hazelnuts
80g Milk Chocolate Java 32%
50g Paillete Feuilletine

DARK CHOCOLATE MOUSSE 'MEXICO'

180g English Cream
3.5g Edible gelatin
110g Dark chocolate Mexico 72%
230g Fresh cream 35%, whipped

CARAMEL AND LIME GLAZE

375g White cane sugar
300g Glucose 42DE
1 Vanilla bean bourbon
450g Fresh cream 35%
4g Lime peel
100g Milk Chocolate Java 32%
18g Gelatine

PROCESS

SPONGE CAKE WITH PISTACHIO

Beat the egg yolks in a planetary mixer with the 100g sugar, separately whisk the egg whites with the 150g sugar, add the two mixtures using a spatula and incorporate the sifted flour and starch without letting the mixture collapse. Separately mix the pistachio paste with one part of the mixture, then add the rest and mix gently. Make discs of 16cm in height with a diameter of 5mm and bake for 6 minutes at 220°C.

GRAND MARNIER BATH

Boil at 60°C the water, sugar and orange peel with the crushed vanilla bean, strain it, and once cooled, add the Grand Marnier liquor.

CREME ANGLAISE
WITH VANILLA BOURBON

In a saucepan place the milk and vanilla and bring to a boil, separately whisk the egg yolks and sugar with a whisk incorporate the eggs into the boiling milk in three parts. Continue to cook mixing together with a whisk. When the cream has thickened (82°C), remove from heat stirring constantly and use in the chocolate cream.

MILK CHOCOLATE CREAM

Pour the hot crème Anglaise over the milk chocolate in small pieces, hazelnut paste and the softened gelatine. Emulsify with a hand blender for 1 minute.

RASPBERRY AND
STRAWBERRY GELATINE

Heat the fruit at 50°C with the lime peel and add the honey. Incorporate the softened gelatine and stir well.

BAVARIAN MASCARPONE

In a saucepan add the egg yolks, sugar, and dextrose, heat at 60°C and put in a planetary mixer to whip. Dissolve softened gelatine and add it to the coffee, incorporating with the whisked mixture, separately mix the mascarpone with the cream and vanilla. Combine the two mixtures first using a fine mesh whip, then with a spatula.

HAZELNUT CRISP

In a container place the caramel coated hazelnuts and milk chocolate melted at 45°C. Using a spoon mix the two ingredients and add the paillete feuilletine stirring constantly. Make discs measuring 16cm in height with a diameter of 5mm and allow to crystallise and reserve.

DARK CHOCOLATE MOUSSE "MEXICO'

Pour the hot English cream over the dark chocolate in small pieces, the fresh cream and the softened gelatin. Blend with a blender with immersion for 1 minute. Fold in the whipped cream first using a fine mesh whip, then with a marisa.

CARAMEL AND LIME GLAZE

In a pan put the sugar, glucose and vanilla and caramelise at 176°C. Reduce with the fresh cream and lime peel. Pour into a container over the milk chocolate and softened gelatine. Emulsify with a hand blender for two minutes, store in the refrigerator at 4°C covered with cling film and use at 30-32°C.

ASSEMBLY

Place one layer of sponge cake with pistachio at the bottom of a 16cm ring and drench with the Grand Marnier bath. Top with milk chocolate cream, then place in a blast freezer. Once frozen pour on a layer of raspberry and strawberry gelatin, place again in a blast freezer and pour in a layer of Bavarian mascarpone. Top with another layer of soaked sponge cake with pistachio and finish freezing. Turn out of the steel ring, pour on a small amount of creamy chocolate and add the hazelnut crisp. Pour into a ring with a diameter of 18cm and 4cm high, insert the inside of the cake into the center of the ring, with the crisp facing down and fill the outside with chocolate mousse. Place in a blast freezer and freeze. Turn out of the steel ring and ice the cake with the caramel and lime glaze.

JAPAN

JAPAN IS A COUNTRY
WHERE THE PAST MEETS
THE FUTURE, COMBINING
TRADITION WITH
MODERNITY, WITH
JAPANESE CULTURE
INCLUDING BOTH RICH
ARTISTIC HERITAGE AS
WELL AS THE LATEST
MODERN FASHIONS
AND TRENDS.

Tokyo, Japan's capital, has more than its fair share of must-see attractions, Imperial Palace, Tokyo Tower, Tokyo Dome City to name a few. Shopping in Tokyo is also an experience to be had, strolling down Shinjuku to find the latest technology or Shibuya and Harajuku to find both the latest fashion trend and witness the Harajuku style fashioned by the Japanese teenagers, styles ranging from Gothic Lolita to 'cute' Kawaii clothing.

It is also essential to experience fresh sushi in Tokyo in one of the many local cafes. Traditional culture can be found in the cities of Kyoto and Nara, experiencing temples, shrines, Kabuki, tea ceremonies and museums. A trip to Japan would not be complete without embracing the modern culture and with the most up to date technology Japan's cities allow visitors to peek into the future of the human race.

"TOKYO, JAPAN'S CAPITAL, HAS MORE THAN ITS FAIR SHARE OF MUST-SEE ATTRACTIONS."

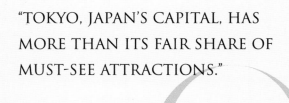

WINNER

YOSHIAKI UEZAKI

JAPAN

YOSHIAKI UEZAKI

The winner of the 2011 World Chocolate Masters Japan national pre-selection Yoshiaki follows in the footsteps of two previous winners as he goes through the 2011 world final representing Japan. Born in the Ibaragi prefecture Yoshiaki has worked in several restaurants and patisseries and is currently sous-chef at Parisserie Kosai. The 2011 Japanese finalist is not a stranger to competitions having won the grand prize for chocolate crafts at the 2006 Japan Cake Show and won gold medals for chocolate showpieces and pastries at at the 2007 Japan Cake Show.

LYCHEE AND STRAWBERRY PRALINE

COATED PRALINE, BY YOSHIAKI UEZAKI MAKES 50

INGREDIENTS

PATES DE FRUIT

132g Raspberry purée
30g Strawberry purée
174g Sugar
4.5g Pectin
48g Starch syrup
48g Strawberry liqueur
1.5g Citric acid
1.5g Water

GANACHE LYCHEE

218g Milk chocolate Callebaut Origine Arriba
68g Dark chocolate Callebaut 3815NV
60g Fresh cream 45%
15g Starch syrup
6g Inverted sugar
82g Lychee liqueur

ROYALTINE FRAISE

225g White Chocolate
90g Royaltine
15g Freeze-dried strawberry

Callebaut 3815NV chocolate, to coat

PROCESS

PATES DE FRUIT

Boil down all ingredients except citric acid and water until the mix reaches 103°C. Add the mixed citric acid and water.

GANACHE LYCHEE

Mix the chocolates and melt together. Heat the fresh cream with starch syrup and inverted sugar, add to the chocolates and mix well until emulsified. Add the lychee liqueur and mix until emulsified.

ROYALTINE FRAISE

Mix all ingredients and spread with 4mm thin.

ASSEMBLY

Spread the pates de fruit 1mm thick in a frame and leave until solidified. When firm pour the ganache onto the pates de fruit 3mm thick and leave it to solidify. Finally add a layer of royaltine fraise 4mm thick and coat in Callebaut 3815NV.

CHERRY BEER PRALINE

MOULDED PRALINE, BY YOSHIAKI UEZAKI MAKES 50

INGREDIENTS

GANACHE LINDEMANS

250g Milk chocolate Callebaut Origine Arriba
70g Dark chocolate Callebaut 3815NV
50g Fresh cream 45%
12g Starch syrup
4g Invert sugar
122g Lindemans cherry beer

GRIOTTES COMPOTE

200g Syrup
30 Griottes, in syrup
40g Kirsch

Callebaut Origine Arriba chocolate, to coat

PROCESS

GANACHE LINDEMANS

Mix the chocolates and melt together.
Heat to 40°C fresh cream with starch syrup
and invert sugar, add to the chocolates and
mix well until emulsified. Add cherry beer,
mix until emulsified.

GRIOTTES COMPOTE

Boil the syrup, add the Griottes and mix
lightly. Add the kirsch.

ASSEMBLY

Coat the moulds with Callebaut Origin
Arriba chocolate and then add the griotte
compote. When cool add the Lindemans
ganache and seal with more Callebaut
Origine Arriba.

EARL GREY AND CASHEW

ENTREMET, BY YOSHIAKI UEZAKI SERVES 6

INGREDIENTS

DACQUOISE NOISETTE

50g Whole hazelnuts
200g Egg white
85g Sugar
40g Trehalose
100g Powdered sugar
15g Flour

BISCUIT CHOCOLAT

250g Egg
14g Invert sugar
135g Sugar
25g Water
100g Flour
20g Cocoa powder
25g Butter

CASHEW NUTS CHOCOLAT

96g Cashew nuts
24g Water
54g Sugar
7g Butter
30g Dark Chocolate Callebaut 3815NV

ROYALTINE CHOCOLAT

14g Whole hazelnuts
14g Hazelnut paste
14g Royaltine
3g Butter
6g Milk Chocolate Callebaut Origine Arriba

CONFI FRAISE

25g Raspberry purée
45g Strawberry purée
40g Sugar
3.2g Jam base
50g Water
10g Strawberry liqueur
10g Kirsch

MOUSSE FRAISE

50g Raspberry purée
80g Strawberry purée
4.2g Gelatin
8g Strawberry liqueur
36g Sugar
15g White chocolate Callebaut W2NV
20g Fresh cheese
80g Fresh cream 38%

CREME EARL GREY

7.8g Earl Grey
100g Milk
24g Frozen egg yolk
30g Sugar
2.7g Gelatin
7g Marsala
100g Mascarpone cheese
72g Fresh cream 38%

MOUSSE CHOCOLAT EARL GREY

13g Earl Grey
264g Milk
6g Gelatin
200g Milk chocolate Callebaut Origine Arriba
380g Fresh cream 38%
80g Dark chocolate Callebaut 3815NV

CHOCOLAT GLAZE

60g Fresh cream 38%
80g Dark chocolate Callebaut 3815NV
50g Praline
180g Neutre
30g Milk
100g Water
50g Water

PROCESS

DACQUOISE NOISETTE

Roast the whole hazelnuts and then crush with a robocoupe. Whip the egg white with sugar and trehalose. Add sieved flour, powders and 100g of the crushed hazelnuts. Pipe them into round 18cm tin and bake for 15 minutes at 180°C.

BISCUIT CHOCOLAT

Whip the whole egg together with invert sugar, sugar and water. Add sieved flour and cocoa powder. Mix with melted butter, spread on a silpat and bake for 7 minutes at 190°C. Cut with a round mould 15cm.

MOUSSE CHOCOLAT EARL GREY

Decoct the Earl Grey with milk and add the soaked gelatin. Mix well with melted chocolate until emulsified. Mix with the whipped fresh cream.

ROYALTINE CHOCOLAT

Crush and mix whole hazelnuts by robot coupe until paste form then mix with hazelnuts paste. Mix with other ingredients.

CONFI FRAISE

Boil all ingredients in the saucepan. Pour into the round mould 15cm with 2mm thin.

MOUSSE FRAISE

Warm all purées, add soaked gelatin, strawberry liquer and sugar. Melt white chocolate and mix with fresh cheese, add to the purées. Mix with fresh cream when it gets cooler.

CREME EARL GREY

Decoct the Earl Grey with milk, mix with egg yolk and sugar to make an Anglaise. Add soaked gelatin and marsala, cool down with chilled water. Add mascarpone. Mix with fresh cream.

CASHEW NUTS CHOCOLAT

Roast cashew nuts and crush roughly. Heat together the water and sugar until it reaches 120°C, add the crushed cashew nuts and mix well. Mix with butter, spread on the baking sheet to cool down. When cold mix with the melted dark chocolate.

CHOCOLAT GLAZE

Add heated fresh cream into dark chocolate to make ganache, add praline and mix. Heat the neutre, milk and 100g water in microwave and add into the ganache. Adjust the hardness with water.

ASSEMBLY

Start with a layer of dacquoise noisette into a tin then add a layer of biscuit chocolat. Cover with a layer of mousse chocolat Earl Grey. Then add the layer of biscuit coated in royaltine chocolate. Then pour the confi fraise 8mm thick onto the biscuit and leave to cool. Then add the mousse frais then place another layer of biscuit chocolat on it, let them solidify. Pour the crème Earl Grey onto the biscuit chocolat 5mm thick. Add a layer of mousse chocolat and 45g of cashew nuts chocolat. Coat with mousse chocolat again and finish with another layer of dacquoise noisette on top. Freeze, remove from the mould and cover with chocolate glaze.

LEBANON

SITUATED IN WESTERN ASIA, ON THE EASTERN SHORE OF THE MEDITERRANEAN, THE LOCATION OF LEBANON HAS DICTATED ITS RICH HISTORY, WHICH IS KNOWN FOR LEAVING MANY VISITORS SPINNING, AND FORMED A CULTURAL IDENTITY OF RELIGIOUS AND ETHNIC DIVERSITY.

Lebanon is renowned for mixing the ancient with the ultramodern making it one of the most captivating countries in the Middle East. With towns like Tripoli (Trablous), famous for its Mamluk architecture and Jounieh, a lively town full of nightclubs and perfect for summer weekends, Lebanon has an array of diverse places to visit and enjoy. Mostly mountainous and with the option of skiing, Lebanon also plays host to a laid-back, liberal and fun atmosphere.

Although Lebanon is not well-known for its chocolate production its passion for chocolate is spread throughout the country. Patchi, a chocolate brand from Lebanon was first established by Nizar Choucair and has more than 140 outlets in 35 countries. The chocolates are unique in style, exquisite in both taste and appearance. So much so that Patchi teamed up with Harrod's to produce the most expensive box of chocolates. The brand includes over 40 varieties of chocolate with recipes mixing almonds, pistachios, hazelnuts with milk or dark chocolate.

"PATCHI, A CHOCOLATE BRAND FROM LEBANON WAS FIRST ESTABLISHED BY NIZAR CHOUCAIR AND HAS MORE THAN 140 OUTLETS IN 35 COUNTRIES."

WINNER

DAMIEN DESLANDES

LEBANON

DAMIEN DESLANDES

Currently Damien is a consultant for the biggest catering company in Lebanon, Faqra Catering. Before that he has been involved in corporate chef sales and been the production manager for advanced baking concept as well as a number of different pastry chef positions. He has a degree from Lenotre in chocolate and cake making and enjoys creating chocolate montages, showpieces and new recipes.

VANILLA AND SESAME PRALINES

COATED PRALINE, BY DAMIEN DESLANDES SERVES 30

INGREDIENTS

VANILLA GANACHE

240g UHT cream
15g Trimoline
4 Vanilla pods
140g Chocolate ganache (55%)
150g Chocolate couverture (66%)
55g Butter

SESAME NOUGATINE

2g Pectin NH
75g Granulated sugar
26g Glucose
60g Butter
60g Golden sesame

Couverture Ganache (Cacoa Barry), to cover

PROCESS

VANILLA GANACHE

Bring the cream and trimoline to the boil and then add the vanilla pods. Leave to infuse for 15 minutes off the heat. Reheat and pour the vanilla cream over the chocolates and emulsify to make a ganache. Stir in the softened butter at 35°C. Pour into a mould at 32°C, leave to crystallise.

SESAME NOUGATINE

Mix the pectin with the sugar. Boil the glucose, sugar, pectin and butter and add the sesame and mix well. Spread on a baking sheet and bake in the oven at 180°C for 10 minutes Cut with a roller.

ASSEMBLY

Pour the vanilla ganache at 32°C into a frame and leave to crystallise. When cool place a one square of sesame nougat on each bonbon. Coat in couverture ganache and leave to set.

HAZELNUT PRALINE

MOULDED PRALINE, BY DAMIEN DESLANDES SERVES 30

INGREDIENTS

HAZELNUT PRALINES

200g Almonds
50g Water
120g Granulated sugar
50g Glucose
20g St Domingue Chocolate 70%
25g Cocoa butter

Elysée milk chocolate couverture, to coat

PROCESS

HAZELNUT PRALINES

Lightly roast the almonds over a medium heat. Boil the water with the sugar and glucose to 130°C. Pour in the warm almonds, continue cooking until browned. Cool and grind.

ASSEMBLY

Temper the melted chocolate couverture with the cocoa butter. Mix with 250g of the hazlenut praline and then pour into moulds. When set fill with hazelnut praline and chill. Then close with the milk chocolate couverture.

AMAZONIE

PLATED DESSERT, BY DAMIEN DESLANDES SERVES 12

INGREDIENTS

TONKA CARAMEL

160g Granulated sugar
160g Single cream
1 Tonka bean, grated
65g Salted butter
60g Butter, softened

CHOCOLATE BISCUIT

100g Beurre Fin (butter from pasteurized cream)
100g Dark chocolate couverture 66%
40g Flour
10g Corn starch
100g Egg whites
100g Granulate sugar

DARK CHOCOLATE MOUSSE

180g Single cream
180g Milk
180g Egg yolks
85g Egg Whites
60g Trimoline
60g Glucose
190g Concorde couverture 66%
170g Whipped cream

VELVET MIX

300g Elysée milk couverture
200g Cocoa butter

PROCESS

TONKA CARAMEL

Caramelise the sugar and add the butters and cream. Then add the tonka bean and heat to 108°C.

CHOCOLATE BISCUIT

Melt the butter and pour onto the couverture, add the sifted flour and corn starch. Beat the egg whites with the sugar until firm and then fold into the chocolate mix. Spread the mixture onto a baking sheet and bake at 190°C. After baking place a portion of the biscuit onto the caramel and reserve the rest for construction.

DARK CHOCOLATE MOUSSE

Add the cream, milk and yolks together and cook as a crème Anglais. Meanwhile make meringue with the egg whites, trimoline and glucose. To make the mousse add 225g of the crème Anglais on to the couverture and mix then add 90g of the meringue mix and the whipped cream and mix until emulsified.

VELVET MIX

Melt and mix the ingredients together.

ASSEMBLY

Flow the caramel tonka into the bottom of a flexipan square, then fill with dark chocolate mousse until the half way. On top of the mousse add a piece of chocolate biscuit and coat with more mousse, then put the last piece of biscuit on top. Freeze for 2 hours then remove from the mould and spray the cake with the velvet mix. Decorate the plate chocolate sauce and a chocolate shell.

CHOCOLATE ORANGE DESSERT

ENTREMET, BY DAMIEN DESLANDES MAKES 3 CAKES, EACH SERVES 6

INGREDIENTS

HAZELNUT DACQUOISE

250g Egg whites
70g Granulated sugar
150g Icing sugar
150g Grey hazelnut powder
100g Blanched hazelnuts, chopped

CHOCOLATE BISCUIT

180g Egg yolks
225g Granulated sugar
270g Egg whites
160g Flour
55g Cocoa powder
55g Fine butter

ORANGE CREAM

185g Orange juice
20g Grand Marnier
Zest of 1 orange
100g Egg yolks
115g Whole eggs
100g Granulated sugar
5g Gelatine powder
30g Cold water
95g Butter

CHOCOLATE MOUSSE

180g Milk
180g Cream
180g Egg yolks
375g Dark chocolate (66%)
225g Meringue
300g Whipped cream

GLAZE

125g Water
300g Granulated sugar
300g Glucose
170g Condensed milk
300g Couverture Papouasie
6g Red colouring, as desired
140g Gelatine

PROCESS

HAZELNUT DACQUOISE

Beat the egg whites with the granulated sugar. Sift the icing sugar together with the hazelnut powder and add the chopped hazelnuts. Pour the icing sugar and nut mixture into the gently beaten egg whites. Arrange on a baking sheet using a chablon (stencil). Bake at 175°C for 20-25 minutes.

ORANGE CREAM

Heat all the ingredients except the butter. Cool to 45/50°C and add the softened butter. Mix the cream without beating.

CHOCOLATE BISCUIT

Beat the egg yolks with two-thirds of the sugar. Beat the egg whites with the remaining sugar. Sift the flour with the cocoa. Melt the butter. Stir the flour and cocoa into the beaten egg yolks, with a quarter of the beaten egg whites. Add the remaining egg whites and then the melted butter. Bake at 180°C for about 45 minutes (bottom shelf).

CHOCOLATE MOUSSE

Cook the cream and milk and when boiled add the egg yolks to make a crème Anglaise, then pour onto the slightly melted chocolate couverture. Mix the meringue in the machine at 35°C and then fold in the whipped cream. Garnish immediately.

GLAZE

Place the water, sugar, glucose and condensed milk on a medium heat and bring to the boil. After boiling, add the coverage the dye and gelatin mass. Mix together and then pass through a chinoise and reserve until needed.

ASSEMBLY

Fill a 16cm ring with hazelnut dacquoise and then layer the chocolate biscuit on top. chill and then add a layer of orange cream and freeze, finally transfer the frozen cake to a 18cm tin and add a layer of chocolate mousse over the top and sides — covering the cake. Freeze and then glaze.

MEXICO

A DIVERSE COUNTRY AND MILLENNIAL CULTURE WITH THE OLMECAN TRIBE BEING THE FIRST CIVILIZATION TO APPEAR AROUND 1500 YEARS BC.

Mexico offers a range of experiences, from the sweaty emerald jungle to the palm-fringed sandy beach. Rich in traditions, history, art and religion Mexico offers a complete tourist infrastructure. Not only that, but dining on salmon enchiladas and chrysanthemum salad at a Mexico City fusion restaurant is a fine way to experience the true Mexican lifestyle which should be accompanied by a night of high energy dancing.

For all the fame of Belgian and Swiss chocolate, one could be forgiven for thinking that they invented the world's favourite treat. However it is Mexico and Central America who should be acknowledged for such universally craved elixir. Although home to the origin of chocolate, very little graces the typical dessert menu and instead it is most commonly used in drinks. There is a fascinating story behind its discovery which started when Spanish explorer Cortés and his men arrived for an audience with Moctezuma in Tenochtitlán in 1519, it was there that they found the Aztec ruler sipping 'bitter water' or xocóatl from golden goblets. The drink was concocted from ground cacao beans boiled in water, then flavored with vanilla and other tropical spices — sugar didn't reach the New World until the Spanish arrived.

"ALTHOUGH HOME TO THE
ORIGIN OF CHOCOLATE, VERY
LITTLE GRACES THE TYPICAL
DESSERT MENU AND INSTEAD
IT IS MOST COMMONLY USED
IN DRINKS. "

WINNER

LUIS ROBLEDO

MEXICO

LUIS ROBLEDO

Luis Robledo is a highly accomplished pastry chef and chocolatier who has learned from and worked with chefs like Daniel Boulud, Francois Payar and Frederic Bau in New York City and Paris before becoming executive pastry chef at Le Cirque and Four Seasons Hotel in New York City. Now back in Mexico, Luis has his own chocolate business, Tout Chocolat, and also has a consulting business (Consorcio Icon).

SECOND PLACE

ALEJANDRO SANTANA

Born in Mexico City, Alejandro has always had a love of chocolate. After furthering his career in bakery and chocolate Alejandro has worked in both hotels and restaurants in Mexico and Paris. Now Alejandro is the pastry sous chef for Hotel Presidente Intercontinental – a prestigious hotel in Mexico City. Alejandro believes that with the appropriate techniques one can transform chocolate to produce multiple forms and textures and that it is the perfect material to create an artistic and esthetic experience.

OSWALDO TAPIA

Oswaldo Tapia studied and specialised in chocolate and confectionary arts at Conseil Bellouet School in Paris, France. He starts his professional career in the Four Seasons Hotel in Mexico City and after that he became Executive Pastry Sous Chef for Le Cirque Restaurant, Mexico City. His passion for chocolate, has take him into many national and international contests, where he has improved his skills and been awarded with many prizes.

RASPBERRY & HAZELNUT CHOCOLATE

COATED PRALINE, BY LUIS ROBLEDO MAKES 36-40

INGREDIENTS

HAZELNUT PRALINE

60g Tanzanian chocolate
25g Cocoa butter
300g Hazelnut praline
15g Feuilletine

FRUIT PASTE

170g Raspberry purée
4g Yellow pectin
190g Sugar
35g Glucose
2g Citric acid

RASPBERRY FILLING

25g Trimoline
100g Raspberry purée
140g Mexican rare Origine chocolate
5g Freeze-dried raspberries
40g Butter

Cacao Barry Guayaquil, to coat
Raspberry gelatine, to decorate

PROCESS

HAZELNUT PRALINE

Mix the chocolate and the cocoa butter and melt at 50°C. Add the praline and mix to a smooth paste. Cool to 26°C and add the feuilletine. Immediately strain into a frame.

FRUIT PASTE

Warm the raspberry purée to 35°C, mix the pectin with the same quantity of sugar bring to the boil, then add the rest of the sugar and glucose. Cook until the mix has reached Brix 72 consistency. Add the citric acid and pour on top of the set praline.

RASPBERRY FILLING

Melt the chocolate to 40°C. Mix the trimoline with the raspberry purée and warm to 45°C. Add the freeze-dried raspberries and emulsify the purée with the chocolate at 45°C. Leave to cool to 35°C. Emulsify with the melted chocolate and add the butter at 35°C. Pour on top of the fruit paste and chill.

ASSEMBLY

Cut fillings to desired size and coat with extra bitter Guayaquil chocolate and decorate with a small ball of raspberry gelatine.

MANDARIN, LEMON & CHOCOLATE BONBON

MOULDED PRALINE, BY LUIS ROBLEDO MAKES 36-40

INGREDIENTS

CITRUS FRUITS CARAMEL

35g Lemon juice
65g Mandarin juice
80g Glucose
100g Cream
1g Vanilla seed
120g Sugar
50g Butter

CHOCOLATE GANACHE

125g Cream
20g Trimoline
2g Vanilla seed
80g Alto el Sol rare Origine chocolate
40g Butter

Cacao Barry Guayaquil, to coat

PROCESS

CITRUS FRUITS CARAMEL

Heat the lemon and mandarin juice. Add the glucose and the cream. Add the vanilla and cover with film to stop it evaporating. Caramelise the sugar, stop it cooking with the hot liquid and then cook to 103°C. Cool down to 35°C and add the butter.

CHOCOLATE GANACHE

Mix the cream, trimoline and vanilla together in a pan. Heat to 45°C and leave to infuse for 10 minutes. Emulsify the cream with the chocolate at 45°C and then cool to 35°C. Add the butter.

ASSEMBLY

Coat the moulds with Guayaquil and set. Pour the caramel into the mould and leave to set. Then top with chocolate ganache and seal with more Guayaquil.

MANDARIN & CHOCOLATE DESSERT

PLATED DESSERT, BY LUIS ROBLEDO SERVES 10

INGREDIENTS

COCOA BEAN ICE CREAM

25g Powdered milk
500g Milk
15g Trimoline
3g Stabiliser
90g Sugar
40g Powdered glucose
30g Egg yolks
200g Cream
125g Cocoa beans

ALTO DE SOL CHOCOLATE CHIBOUST CREAM

170g Alto el Sol chocolate
85g Milk
85g Cream
55g Egg yolks
60g Sugar
10g Cornstarch
133g Egg whites
20g Sugar

CHOCOLATE JELLY

20g Sugar
8g Pectin X58
300g Milk
80g Venezuelan rare Origine chocolate

WHIPPED GANACHE

90g Cream
10g Glucose
10g Trimoline
80g Chocolate 72%
185g Cream

STREUSEL

50g Muscovado sugar
50g Flour
50g Butter
50g Almond powder

MANDARIN COMPOTE

200g Fresh mandarins
1g Vanilla seeds
0.5g Verveine
3g Yellow pectin
25g Sugar

GRUE DE COCOA FOAM

25g Grue de Cocoa
200g Milk
1g Gelatine
50g Cream
20g Sugar

GRUE DE COCOA NOUGATINE

75g Sugar
2g NH Pectin
120g Butter
50g Glucose
10g Water
15g Grue de Cocoa

PROCESS

COCOA BEAN ICE CREAM

Mix the milk and the dry milk, warm up to 33°C and add the trimoline and stablizer, warm to 40°C and add the glucose and sugar. Heat the mix to 50°C and then add the yolks and cream. Add the Grue de Cocoa Nougatine and cook to 84°C. Blend and strain over an ice bath and leave to rest for a couple of hours. Then process in an ice cream machine.

ALTO DE SOL CHOCOLATE CHIBOUST CREAM

Melt the chocolate at 50°C. Make a crème pâtissière with the milk, cream, egg yolks, sugar and cornstarch. Whip the egg whites with the sugar. Emulsify a third of the whipped egg whites with the chocolate at 50°C. Add the hot crème pâtissière and continue to emulsify. Add the whipped egg whites carefully and empty into 3cm cake rings. Freeze.

CHOCOLATE JELLY

Mix the sugar and the X58. Heat the milk to 30°C and drop the sugar pectin combo in. Boil. Pour over the chocolate and emulsify little by little. Strain and refrigerate in 4cm moulds.

WHIPPED GANACHE

Emulsify the 90g cream, glucose, trimoline and chocolate at 45°C. Add the 185g cream (cooled). Keep in the fridge and whip in a mixer just before serving.

STREUSEL

Mix all the ingredients with the spatula until grainy. Cook at 160°C for 20 minutes.

MANDARIN COMPOTE

Mix the mandarins with the vanilla and the verveine. Take a small amount of the mandarin juice and heat to 35°C. Mix the pectin and sugar and pour in. Boil for 2 minutes and keep in the fridge.

GRUE DE COCOA FOAM

Roast the grue de cocoa for 8 minutes at 180°C, warm up the milk and sugar and add the the cocoa nibs to infuse. Strain and reweigh once more and retain 200g. Incorporate the previously softened gelatine. Add the cream and sugar. Load the siphon and refrigerate until use.

GRUE DE COCOA NOUGATINE

Mix the sugar and pectin in a pan, then add the butter, glucose and the water. Boil until completely smooth. Remove from the heat and add the cocoa beans. Roll out on a silpat and bake at 200°C until firm then cut out a disc around 4cm.

ASSEMBLY

Make a chocolate cylinder 3 x 10cm using extra bitter Guayaquil. Fill the cylinder with one-third streusel, one-third mandarin compote and one-third ganache. Finally add the cocoa nib foam on the top. Decorate the plate with streusel and a quenelle of ice cream, some more mandarin compote and the nougatine disc with the chocolate jelly on top.

CHOCOLATE CAKE WITH FRUITS FROM THE COCOA LANDS

ENTREMET, BY LUIS ROBLEDO MAKES 2 CAKES, EACH SERVES 8

INGREDIENTS

CRISPY STREUSEL

265g Butter
265g Sugar
2g Salt
300g Powdered almonds
285g Flour

NUT & COCOA BEAN CRISP

40g Ghanaian chocolate
40g Butter
170g Almond praline
90g Toasted almonds
75g Toasted hazelnuts
65g Toasted cocoa beans

ALMOND DACQUOISE

20g Flour
385g Icing
385g Almond
400g Egg whites
2g Cream of tartar
160g Sugar

CREAM OF TROPICAL FRUITS

4g Gelatine
250g Tropical fruit purée
150g Eggs
120g Egg yolks
150g Sugar
120g Butter

'MEXICAN RARE ORIGINE' CHOCOLATE CREAM

220g Pouring cream 35% MG
220g Whole milk
80g Egg yolks
40g Sugar
230g Mexican rare Origine chocolate

SMOOTH CHOCOLATE BISCUIT

385g Venezuelan rare Origine chocolate
200g Butter
200g Egg yolks
380g Egg whites
210g Sugar
75g Flour

GRUE DE COCOA MOUSSE

80g Grue de Cocoa
350g Milk
300g Cream
80g Egg yolks
80g Sugar
14g Gelatine
340g Cream

PROCESS

CRISPY STREUSEL

Soften the butter, add the rest of the ingredients and mix gently until a smooth paste is achieved. Cut, refrigerate and bake at 180°C for 20 minutes.

NUT & COCOA BEAN CRISP

Melt the chocolate and the butter, add the praline, add the dried nuts and the toasted cocoa beans. Pour into a mould and freeze.

ALMOND DACQUOISE

Sieve the dried ingredients except the cream of tartar and sugar. Whip the egg whites with the cream of tartar and the sugar. Mix both together and roll out on a silpat. Bake at 170°C until 10 or 15 just before golden.

CREAM OF TROPICAL FRUITS

Soften the gelatine in cold water. Mix the purée, the eggs, egg yolks and sugar in a small pan. Bring slowly to the boil, add the gelatine and strain through a fine sieve. Cool to 35°C and add the butter. Pour into moulds and freeze.

'MEXICAN RARE ORIGINE' CHOCOLATE CREAM

Make a crème Anglaise with the first four ingredients and cook to 84°C. Emulsify with the chocolate and pour into a ring. Freeze.

SMOOTH CHOCOLATE BISCUIT

Melt the chocolate with the butter. Add the egg yolks and whip the egg whites with the sugar, emulsify one-third of the egg whites with the chocolate mixture and all the flour and delicately fold in the egg whites and the flour. Cook on a silpat at 180°C for 10-15 minutes.

GRUE DE COCOA MOUSSE

Bake the grue de cocoa for 6 minutes in the oven at 160°C. Pour over the milk and the cream. Leave to infuse for 10 minutes (covered with film). Using the infused liquid, make a crème Anglaise with the egg yolks and sugar. Add the previously softened gelatine and strain the crème Anglaise. Cool to 33°C and gently add the whipped cream.

ASSEMBLY

Place into a 9cm cake frame and layer first with streusel, the nut and cocoa crisp, then a layer of chocolate biscuit, then chocolate cream, the cream of tropical fruit, then almond dacquoise then remove from the tin and cut slightly smaller than the tin and replace back in the frame. Then cover with chocolate mousse completely covering the cake and freeze, dust with cocoa and decorate as desired.

NETHERLANDS

A SMALL COUNTRY WITH A BIG PROFILE, THE NETHERLANDS HAS A LOT TO OFFER, FROM ALLURING SCENERY TO THE VIBRANT CULTURE OF AMSTERDAM, KNOWN FOR ITS ARRAY OF COFFEE SHOPS AND CANALS.

There are also the stunning metropoles of Haarlem, Rotterdam, Leiden, Delft, Maastricht and Den Haag that are only hours or even minutes away by train. There aren't many – if any – countries this flat, making it an ideal destination for cycling, an integral mode of transport among the Dutch themselves. Also, outside of the major cities, there is a rural splendour of national parks where it wouldn't be unusual to find a shimmering lake and other natural beauties. The Netherlands also plays host to sandy coastlines and a chain of windswept islands, leaving the visitor with a variety of things to see and do.

Dutch chocolate is different to most by the fact that Dutch chocolate is actually the name for a process known as 'dutching' which is the removal of cocoa butter from cocoa beans. The cocoa is then treated with an alkalizing agent to improve the colour and flavour. Dutch chocolate forms the basis for a lot of chocolate candy, ice cream, and baking cocoa.

"DUTCH CHOCOLATE IS ACTUALLY THE NAME FOR A PROCESS KNOWN AS 'DUTCHING' WHICH IS THE REMOVAL OF COCOA BUTTER FROM COCOA BEANS."

WINNER

FRANK HAASNOOT

NETHERLANDS

FRANK HAASNOOT

After Frank Haasnoot graduated from a course in pastry arts' in Amsterdam, he started his career as pastry chef at La Tulipe Desserts in New York in 2001. Throughout the years he has worked at pastry shops, restaurants and hotels. This is Frank's second time at the World Chocolate Masters as he won the Dutch heat in 2007 and in 2009 represented the Netherlands at the World Chocolate Masters in Paris, where he gained the fourth place. At this moment Frank Haasnoot is the executive pastry chef at Dobla.

SECOND PLACE

DANIEL JONGSMA

Daniël Jongsma started his career by studying pastry at ROC in Amsterdam. Since graduating he has finished several courses in ice and advanced sugar techniques. Last year Daniël won the Dutch Pastry Awards and the price for best newcomer. At this moment he is working at Passionelle Tummers in Heemstede.

THIRD PLACE

RENE HUISMAN

Rene Huisman was born in Amsterdam, Netherlands and has a bakery in Leeuwarden where he is a chocolatier. His bakery encourages him to be creative and this is where he practices for the competition. Rene decided to take part in the Netherlands Chocolate Masters as he is dedicated to showing how people can be inspired by chocolate. For Rene meeting people and being involved was the best part of the competition.

MONARCH

COATED PRALINE, BY FRANK HAASNOOT MAKES 50

INGREDIENTS

BANANA NUTMEG GANACHE

200g Cream
350g Ripe banana
1g Nutmeg
700g Pure chocolate Mexico 66% (Cacao
Barry), melted
90g Invert sugar [trimoline]
150g Butter

CASHEW CRISP

30g Milk chocolate Elysee 36% (Cacao
Barry)
25g Cocoa butter
130g Salted cashew paste
140g Chopped salted cashews
140g Feuilletine
270g Praline Heritage (Cacao Barry)
0.5g Ground pepper
0.5g Sea salt

Pure chocolate 811, to coat
Wafer butterfly

PROCESS

BANANA NUTMEG GANACHE

Bring the cream, ripe banana and nutmeg
to the boil and blend till smooth with a
handheld blender. Sieve into the melted
chocolate and invert sugar. Add butter at
45°C and blend.

CASHEW CRISP

Melt the milk chocolate and cocoa butter
and mix with the other ingredients.

ASSEMBLY

Using a frame make a base of dark
chocolate 811. Then add the banana
ganache and cool. On top of that add the
cashew crisp and chill. Cut to size and dip
the chocolates in dark chocolate 811.

PASSION FLOWERS

MOULDED PRALINE, FRANK HAASNOOT MAKES 50

INGREDIENTS

MARSHMALLOW

60g Sugar
20g Glucose
20g Dextrose
5g Gelatine
25g Water
Lime zest, to taste

PASSION MINT CARAMEL

180g Sugar
120g Glucose
300g Passionfruit coulis
150g Milk chocolate Elysee 36 % (Cacao Barry)
50g Honey
75g Butter
7g Fresh mint

Pure chocolate 811, to coat

PROCESS

MARSHMALLOW

Soak the gelatine. Bring the sugar and dextrose to the boil. Pour the boiling liquid onto the glucose. Add the bloomed gelatine. Whisk until there is three times the amount and pipe into the moulds.

PASSION MINT CARAMEL

Heat the passionfruit coulis and add the mint. Caramelise the sugar and then add the sieved passionfruit coulis to the caramel, then add the honey. Add the milk chocolate and emulsify. Add the butter at between 35°C and 40°C. Fill the moulds at 29°C.

ASSEMBLY

Coat the moulds in dark chocolate 811 and then leave to harden. Add the marshmallow filling and leave to set. Then add the mint caramel and leave to set. When cool coat with more dark chocolate 811.

AZTEC RITUAL

PLATED DESSERT, BY FRANK HAASNOOT SERVES 6

INGREDIENTS

CHOCOLATE TONKA MOUSSE

110g Whipping cream
50g Chocolate Saint-Domingue 70% (Cacao Barry)
25g Egg yolk
25g Sugar
45g Milk
2g Gelatine
8g Water
5g Tonka beans
25g Crème de Cacao 17%

CHOCOLATE CRUMBLE

13g Cocoa powder
50g Almond powder
38g Patent flour
50g Cane sugar
38g Butter
13g Chocolate Saint-Domingue 70% (Cacao Barry)

CHOCOLATE FOAM

85g Water
50g Crème de Cacao 17%
75g Cocoa Nibs (Callebaut)
50g Sugar
½ Vanilla pod
20g Albumin

COCONUT PARFAIT

90g Cane sugar
50g Egg yolk
84g Coconut purée
15g Malibu
200g Cream, whipped
200g Chocolate Mexico 66% (Cacao Barry)
50g Oil

PASSION CREMEA

100g Crème dell' Artigiano glaze (Callebaut)
35g Passionfruit juice
15g Mango purée
10g Mango vinegar

1 Fresh mango, cut into blocks
Lime Cress
Chrispie pinge (available from sosa)
Green leaves

PROCESS

CHOCOLATE TONKA MOUSSE

Heat the sugar with a little water to 120°C and mix with the egg yolk. Whisk it to an airy finish like a pâte à bombe. Soak the gelatine in the water and when bloomed add to the melted chocolate. Boil the Tonka beans and the milk and leave to rest for half an hour. Whip the whipping cream to soft peaks. Bring the milk and Tonka beans to the boil again and strain above the gelatine and chocolate. Mix this into a ganache. Mix the ganache with the pâte à bombe and then with the whipped cream.

CHOCOLATE CRUMBLE

Mix the cocoa powder, almond powder, patent flour and cane sugar. Melt the butter and chocolate and mix with the dry ingredients. Bake at 180°C for approximately 20 minutes.

CHOCOLATE FOAM

Bring the water, Crème de Cacao, Cocoa Nibs, sugar and vanilla pod to the boil and leave to soak for half an hour. Then whisk together with albumin until airy. Pipe onto baking trays and dry at 60°C till crispy.

COCONUT PARFAIT

Heat the cane sugar and a little water to 120°C and mix well with the egg yolk. Whisk till airy, like a pâte à bombe. Whip the cream into soft peaks. Mix the coconut purée with the Malibu and add this to the pâte à bombe. Now mix with the whipped cream. Freeze and then cut coconut shaped pieces from the parfait mix. Roll one side in the melted chocolate and oil mix and leave to cool.

PASSION CREMEA

Mix all ingredients thoroughly with a handheld blender.

ASSEMBLY

Lay all the components on a plate as pictured.

SACRIFICE

ENTREMET, BY FRANK HAASNOOT MAKES 2 CAKES, EACH SERVES 8-10

INGREDIENTS

CHOCOLATE TONKA MOUSSE

85g Sugar
40g Water
85g Egg yolk
8g Gelatine
200g Chocolate Saint Domingue 70%
(Cacao Barry)
20g Tonka beans
400g Whipping cream
175g Milk

CARDAMOM VANILLA FOAM

120g Orange juice
0.3g Cardamom
½ Vanilla pod
2.4g Gelatine
20g Water
12g Albumin
90g Sugar

FEUILLETINE CRISP

95g Milk Chocolate Elysee 36% (Cacao Barry)
125g Praline Heritage (Cacao Barry)
75g Feuilletine (Callebaut)
1½g Candied orange peel
3g Sea salt

CARAMEL PRALINE

125g Cream
205g Praline PNP-666 Hazelnut (Callebaut)
55g Sugar
25g Butter
3g Sea salt

ALMOND BISCUIT

290g Egg
200g Almond powder
40g Sugar
2g Salt
165g Egg white
200g Sugar
36g Butter, melted
3g Cream powder, sieved
64g Patent flour

CHOCOLATE ALMOND BISCUIT

290g Egg
200g Almond powder
2g Salt
40g Sugar
165g Egg white
200g Sugar
36g Butter, melted
3g Cream powder, sieved
32g Cocoa powder (Callebaut)
32g Patent flour

Choc O'shine (Callebaut), to coat

PROCESS

CHOCOLATE TONKA MOUSSE

Heat the sugar with a little water to 120°C and mix with the egg yolk. Whisk it to an airy finish like a pâte à bombe. Soak the gelatine in the water and when bloomed add to the melted chocolate. Boil the Tonka beans and the milk and leave to rest for half an hour. Whip the whipping cream to soft peaks. Bring the milk and Tonka beans to the boil again and strain above the gelatine and chocolate. Mix this into a ganache. Mix the ganache with the pâte à bombe and then with the whipped cream.

CARDAMOM VANILLA FOAM

Bring the orange juice to a boil and soak the cardamom and vanilla pod. Soak the gelatine in the water. Mix the albumin and sugar together. Bring the orange juice to the boil again and strain it over the albumin. Whisk to an airy finish. Heat the gelatine and mix with the airy orange foam.

FEUILLETINE CRISP

Melt the milk chocolate and mix with the other ingredients.

CARAMEL PRALINE

Caramelise the sugar and cool with butter and cream. Mix this with the praline.

ALMOND BISCUIT

Mix the eggs, almond powder, salt and the smaller amount of sugar together. Whisk the egg white until airy with the larger amount of sugar. Mix the egg white foam with the egg yolk mixture. Stir in the melted butter. Spoon the sieved cream powder and patent flour through the mixture. Bake at 230°C for approximately 7 minutes.

CHOCOLATE ALMOND BISCUIT

Mix the eggs, almond powder, salt and smaller amount of sugar. Whisk the egg white till airy with the larger amount of sugar. Mix the egg white foam with the egg yolk mixture. Stir in the melted butter. Spoon in the sieved cream powder, cocoa powder and patent flour. Bake at 210°C for approximately 10 minutes.

ASSEMBLY

In a 20cm ring, first fill a layer of chocolate tonka mousse, then a layer of almond biscuit, then a layer of cardamom foam, and almond biscuit again, then another layer of tonka mousse, then the chocolate almond biscuit, then the caramel praline finally the feuillitine crisp. If necessary freeze each layer before starting the next, finally freeze the cake until firm and then remove and glaze at 38°C.

RUSSIA

AT 6,592,800 SQUARE MILES AND WITH A POPULATION OF 143 MILLION, RUSSIA IS BY FAR THE LARGEST COUNTRY IN THE WORLD AND COVERS MORE THAN A NINTH OF THE EARTH'S LAND AREA.

Renowned as the land of the riches, Russia has a wealthy past and a promising future. Russia is made up of a diverse range of landscapes and scenery from snow-capped mountains to beautiful beaches. Visitors, if exploring a little deeper, will find ancient fortresses and hidden villages.

Playing host to big name cities such as Moscow and St Petersburg, Russia has plenty to see and do, and iconic sights so breathtaking visitors will spend days in awe. The world's oldest and deepest lake, Lake Baikal, is an unforgettable sight and the most outstanding example of fresh water. Those who look a little further will find a whole host of undiscovered secrets. The chocolate tradition in Russia is like nowhere else in the world. Russian chocolate sweets are said to be truly unique and some of the best are made in 'Babaevsky' and 'Red October' factories, with Babaevsky concern being the oldest confectionary factory in Russia.

"THE CHOCOLATE TRADITION IN RUSSIA IS LIKE NOWHERE ELSE IN THE WORLD."

WINNER

ALEKSANDER ILYUKHIN

RUSSIA

ALEKSANDER ILYUKHIN

Alex Llyukhin studied at the Moscow Insititute of Corporate Management but has undertaken many additional culinary courses including a Ravifruit master class and individual courses with Moscow Academy of Gastronomy. As well as becoming the finalist for Russia in the 2006 World Chocolate Master heats, Alex continued through to World Chocolate Master Final in Paris. At present Alex is the pastry chef at Le Khleb bakery, but has also worked at the Renaissance Moscow Hotel and the Centre of Culinary Arts.

JOINT SECOND PLACE
GLUSHKOV ARTEM

For Artem Glushkov, his desire to learn and to discover new skills made the World Chocolate Masters Russian final a must-enter competition. His first competition Artem works in the restaurant 'SOHO' as a manager and head chef. Eager to break into the international world of pastry art and chocolate he has studied for the competition and is inspired by the other contestants and their creations which has given him passion to compete more in the future.

JOINT SECOND PLACE
ALEX SCHIKAREV

Alex Schikarev currently works at the Centre of Education 'Laboratory of Flavour' as a brand-chef. He has a great deal of experience in chocolate having entered a great number of competitions before the Russian final of the World Chocolate Masters. Previously he has been awarded as a gold prize winner for the World Cup (Cusine Salon) in Turkey and 2010 competition in Luxembourg. He is also a gold prize winner from the International Cusines Salon in Eurasia 2009. Alex has a strong interest in show pieces and new ideas for chocolate which is why he chose to enter the World Chocolate Master competition.

CHOCOLATE BERRY PRALINE

COATED PRALINE, BY ALEKSANDER ILYUKHIN MAKES 30

INGREDIENTS

THREE-NUT FILLING

110g Whole hazelnuts
110g Whole almonds
110g Whole pistachios
80g Water
165g Sugar
50g Invert sugar

FRUIT JELLY

95g Raspberry purée
95g Blackberry purée
95g Strawberry purée
95g Redcurrants
50g Glucose
50g Invert sugar
50g Sugar
4g Pectin

CHOCOLATE GANACHE

160g Cream 35% fat
23g Invert sugar
228g Bitter chocolate 70 30 38 Cacao Barry

Bitter chocolate 70 30 38 Cacao Barry, to coat

PROCESS

THREE-NUT FILLING

Chop the nuts into small pieces. Heat the water, sugar and invert sugar to 117°C until it makes a syrup. Mix the chopped nuts with the syrup, blend and reduce some of the oil from the mix using a press. Roll out the mix into a thin layer with a rolling pin and leave to cool on a silpat mat.

FRUIT JELLY

Mix the purées and redcurrants, glucose and invert sugar then bring to the boil and add the sugar and pectin. Stir while boiling for approximately 10 minutes.

CHOCOLATE GANACHE

Bring the cream to the boil with the invert sugar, mix with the chocolate then cool to 32°C and blend.

ASSEMBLY

In a frame lay the nut filling and fill with the fruit jelly and chill. When set finish the frame with the ganache and chill. Cut and coat with bitter chocolate.

EXOTIC PRALINE
MOULDED PRALINE, BY ALEKSANDER ILYUKHIN MAKES 30

INGREDIENTS

ARTISAN ALMOND PRALINE

50g Water
125g Sugar
75g Glucose
1.5g Vanilla pod
325g Whole almonds

EXOTIC FILLING

100g Exotic purée
320g Milk chocolate
85g Cream 35% fat

Cacao Barry bitter chocolate 70 30 38, to coat

PROCESS

ARTISAN ALMOND PRALINE

Make a syrup of water, sugar, glucose and vanilla and roast the almonds in the syrup until they become a golden. Cool and then blend to a liquid consistency and cool again.

EXOTIC FILLING

Heat the purée and mix with the melted chocolate then add the cream. Blend and allow to cool.

ASSEMBLY

Coat the moulds with bitter chocolate and cool. Then fill with almond praline and cool, then add the exotic filling and cool before sealing with more bitter chocolate.

BLACKCURRANT CHOCOLATE

ENTREMET, BY ALEKSANDER ILYUKHIN MAKES 2 CAKES, EACH SERVES 10-12

INGREDIENTS

HAZELNUT STREUSEL

100g Hazelnuts, chopped
100g Wheat flour
100g Butter
100g Sugar

CHOCOLATE MOUSSE

50g Sugar
30g Water
75g Egg yolks
40g Eggs
4g Gelatine
162g Bitter chocolate
250g Whipped cream 35% fat
50g Blackcurrant liquor

CHEESE CREAM

135g Cream
130g Milk chocolate Papouasie (Cacao Barry)
150g Cream cheese

CHOCOLATE FLOURLESS BISCUIT

230g Egg whites
5g Dry egg whites
220g Sugar
150g Egg yolks
80g Cacao powder

BLACKCURRANT FRUIT JELLY

380g Blackcurrant purée
50g Glucose
25g Invert sugar
50g Sugar
4g Pectin

CHOCOLATE SHINE GLAZE

150g Cream 38%
75g Water
85g Cocoa powder
200g Sugar
15g Gelatin

PROCESS

HAZELNUT STREUSEL

Mix all the ingredients. Place on a silpat and bake at 180°C until a golden colour.

CHOCOLATE MOUSSE

Boil together the sugar and water to make a syrup. Mix together the egg yolks, eggs and syrup. Fold in the gelatine, melted chocolate, whipped cream and liquor. Mix to a homogeneous mass.

CHEESE CREAM

Mix the hot cream with the chocolate, then cool. Add the cream cheese and blend until mixed.

CHOCOLATE FLOURLESS BISCUIT

Whip both types of egg whites with the sugar then add the whipped egg yolks. Carefully add the cacao powder. Mix together thoroughly. Bake at 150°C for 10 minutes and then cool.

BLACKCURRANT FRUIT JELLY

Mix together the purée, glucose, invert sugar and bring to the boil. Add the sugar and pectin. Boil for 10 minutes.

CHOCOLATE SHINE GLAZE

Mix all the ingredients but the gelatine and boil to 101°C. Cool to 60°C and add the gelatine and cool to 30°C before coating.

ASSEMBLY

In a layer the streusel on the bottom and then add a layer of mousse and chill. When cold add a layer of cheese cream and chill. On top of this add a thin layer of biscuit and then a layer of blackvurrant fruit jelly And then add another layer of biscuit and then another layer of cheese cream . Chill and then remove from the mould and cover entirely with mousse, smooth and freeze. When frozen coat with chocolate shine glaze.

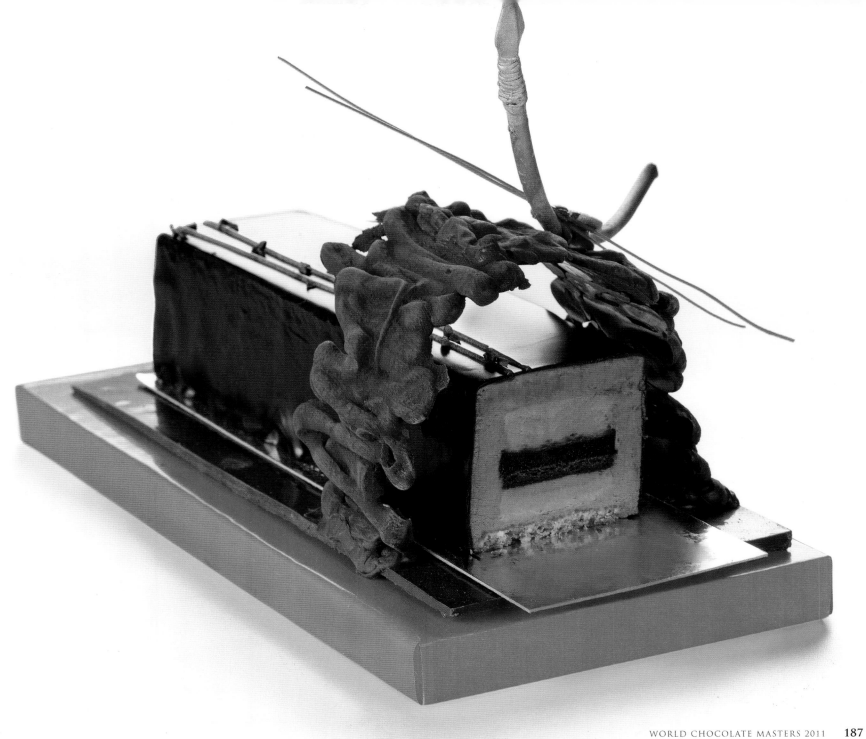

SPAIN

KNOWN FOR ITS GREAT PANS OF STEAMING PAELLA AND PITCHERS OF SANGRIA, THERE IS A VIBRANT IMAGE ASSOCIATED WITH SPAIN.

However beyond these clichéd images, there is a vast amount that Spain has to offer. Not only is Spain littered with glittering beaches, you will also find a scattering of medieval towns, emerald green mountains and lively cities. Barcelona is considered Spain's most cosmopolitan city and features one of the Mediterranean's busiest ports. From the marvels of modernism to the modern wonders of today, Barcelona is renowned for its artistic flare, architecture and style since the late 19th century. Spain's capital, Madrid, combines everything from astonishing art galleries to a city known for exceptional live music and a nightlife like no other – Madrid is made up of a population that's mastered the art of living the good life.

In terms of chocolate, the Spanish are renowned for taking chocolate in a direction that the Mayans and Aztecs did not consider, all with the addition of cane sugar. Once the rest of Europe tasted this new drink, it became a fad that swept across the continent. Since the time of its discovery, the Spanish have been obsessed with chocolate. Chocolate drinking establishments are called chocolaterias in Spain and serve the sweet, rich beverage, as well as cakes and pastries to accompany it. So enamored were the Madrilenos with the drink that the Pope was asked to change the rules regarding fasting to exclude chocolate. To this day, chocolate is a standard breakfast drink, especially in Madrid. Chocolate con Churros (Hot Chocolate with Fritters) is a popular breakfast around Spain.

"THE SPANISH ARE
RENOWNED FOR TAKING
CHOCOLATE IN A DIRECTION
THAT THE MAYANS AND AZTECS
DID NOT CONSIDER."

WINNER

FRANCISCO JOSE SOMOZA ESTEVEZ

SPAIN

FRANCISCO JOSE SOMOZA ESTEVEZ

Francisco has taken part in many competitions previous to the World Chocolate Masters including being voted Best Spanish Pastry Chef in 2007 and obtaining a medal for a competition from the Spanish Chamber of Commerce for one of his desserts. As well as working as a pastry chef, Francisco combines his time by teaching in training centres and working as an ambassador for Vergers Boiron and KenEuropa in Spain.

SECOND PLACE

SALVADOR GARCIA MORENO

Salvador Garcia lives in Terrassa (Barcelona) and he currently works for the company GB Plange in the R & D department. He strives to beat his personal best and enjoys pushing himself to the limit when taking part in the competition. As well as taking part in many competitions Salvador has previously taken part in the Spanish preselections for the World Chocolate Masters 2009 where he came third.

THIRD PLACE

ANDRES MARMOL MARTINEZ

Andrés Mármol he is the owner of the Pastelería y Confitería la Gloria, SL and currently lives in El Palmar (Murcia). He likes working with chocolate and he thinks that participating will show him new methods of working with chocolate. He participated in the contest Lluís Santapau 2008 and came third place and has also won the competition Postre Infanta Leonor 2006.

NECTAR OF FRESH LIME & COCONUT
COATED PRALINE, BY FRANCISCO JOSE SOMOZA ESTEVEZ SERVES 40

INGREDIENTS

TROPICAL GANACHE

25g UHT cream 35% mg
250g Coconut purée
25g Glucose 40 DE
450g Blanc Satin couverture
50g Cocoa butter
1 Fresh lime, grated
1g Nutmeg, grated
1g Salt
25g Coconut, grated

LIME JELLY

70g Lime juice
105g Water
220g Sucrose
7g Yellow pectin
33g Glucose
17g Invert sugar
4g Citric acid 50% (+4 grams H2O)

Dark chocolate 811, to coat
Yellow and green cocoa butter, for the base
Blanc Satin couverture, for the base

PROCESS

TROPICAL GANACHE

Bring the liquids (cream and coconut purée) to the boil together with the glucose. Pour over the couverture and the cocoa butter. Ad the spice and season the lime, nutmeg and salt. Emulsify in the Thermomix and heat to 28°C.

LIME JELLY

Warm the juice and water. Mix together the sucrose and the pectin and add to the liquid. Once these ingredients have dissolved, blend in the invert sugar and the glucose. Regulate the temperature and when it reaches 105°C, add the citric acid solution.

ASSEMBLY

Pour the tropical ganache into a frame and leave to cool for 24 hours. Pour the lime jelly on top and leave to cool. Cut with a guitar cutter into 25 x 25 mm squares.

Sprinkle a silpat with green and yellow-coloured cocoa butter warmed to 29°C and coat with white chocolate. Cut 25mm squares and make a hole in the centre with a flat metal nozzle no. 6. Coat in dark chocolate and then place a square on the bonbon.

RED PEPPER PRALINE

MOULDED PRALINE, BY FRANCISCO JOSE SOMOZA ESTEVEZ SERVES 40

INGREDIENTS

PEPPER GANACHE

175g Pepper purée
210g Sugar
175g Raspberry purée
88g UHT cream 35% mg
438g Barry Lactée couverture
88g Butter

ROASTED RED PEPPER MARMALADE

400g Red cristal peppers
oil, for roasting
200g Granulated sugar
50g Lemon or lime juice

Red and gold cocoa butter, to decorate
Dark Guayaquil, to coat

PROCESS

PEPPER GANACHE

Firstly, liquidise the red peppers to make 750g pepper juice, then reduce it until it makes 175g required for the recipe. Brown the sugar and de-glaze with the hot purée and cream. Pour over the couverture and emulsify. Lastly, add the butter. Place in moulds at 30°C.

ROASTED RED PEPPER MARMALADE

Wash the peppers. Coat them lightly with oil then splash in water before placing in an oven at 200°C and remove before they start to roast (when the skin starts to come away). Once peeled, place in the Thermomix, process first and then put on the butterfly and cook steam (vahrona) together with the sugar. When it is almost cooked, add the lemon juice. Check that the degree brix is 60 so that it stays fresh.

ASSEMBLY

Coat the cocoa bean moulds with splashes of gold and red cocoa butter and then coat with dark couverture. Fill the mould half with marmalade and leave to cool, then add the ganache and leave to set. Coat with a layer of dark chocolate to seal.

LIQUORICE & PINEAPPLE FLOWER WITH CHOCOLATE

PLATED DESSERT, BY FRANCISCO JOSE SOMOZA ESTEVEZ SERVES 6

INGREDIENTS

MOIST CHOCOLATE SPONGE CAKE

200g Butter
240g Sugar
4g Salt
120g Dark couverture 60-70%
160g Eggs
140g Pastry flour

CHOCOLATE CREAM

250g Cream
50g Sugar
80g Egg yolks
70g Dark couverture 811
3 sheets Gelatine

CHOCOLATE CRISP

40g Butter
40g Orange juice
100g Icing sugar
1g Powdered liquorice
32g Flour T-55 (strong)
10g Cocoa

MASCARPONE AND LIQUORICE ICE CREAM

578g Whole milk
170g Mascarpone cheese
29g Cream 35%
24g Skimmed powdered milk
Liquorice, as desired
177g Dextrose
2g Salt
20g Saccharose
Stabilizer, as needed

PINEAPPLE FLOWER

250g Pineapple purée
2g Agar agar
3g Gelatine
White chocolate Blanc Satin, as needed

SAUTÉED PINEAPPLE CUBES

20 pieces Very ripe pineapple
Mycryo, to coat the pieces
Mature rum, to sauté
Vanilla, to taste

CANDIED PINE NUTS

30g Water
100g Sugar
200g Raw pine nuts
Gold powder

SEMI-CANDIED CHESTNUTS

250g Chestnuts
200g Sugar
200g Water
20g Aniseed seeds
5g sprig of licorice

VIOLET SAUCE

Unflavoured gelatine, as needed
Violet oil, as needed
Violet petals, as needed

PROCESS

MOIST CHOCOLATE SPONGE CAKE

Whip the butter with the sugar and the salt. Add the melted couverture. Gradually add the eggs. Lastly, add the flour, cook at 180°C for 10 minutes.

CHOCOLATE CREAM

Place the cream, sugar and the egg yolks in the Thermomix. Set to 85°C, speed setting 3, for 6 minutes. Add the couverture and the softened gelatine sheets. Using the dosing unit, stick mini quenelles on the flexipan. Decorate with a griottine. Freeze.

CHOCOLATE CRISP

Mix the melted butter and the juice with a spatula. Sieve and add the icing sugar, liquorice the flour and the cocoa. Make a thin layer on the silpat and cook at 180°C for 7 minutes. Cut out with a silicone leaf mould when it comes out of the oven to give it shape.

MASCARPONE AND LIQUORICE ICE CREAM

Place the warm milk, mascarpone, cream, skimmed powdered milk, powdered licorice, dextrose and salt in the Thermomix. Heat to 35°C. Mix the saccharose and the stabilizer together and add to the above. Heat to 85°C then cool and store in the fridge. Leave for 24 hours.

PINEAPPLE FLOWER

Heat the purée and the agar agar to 85°C. Add the softened gelatine and shape into balls. Sprinkle with white chocolate blanc satin and make into a flower shape.

SAUTÉED PINEAPPLE CUBES

Cut into cubes, coat in Mycryo and sauté. Add the rum and the vanilla and keep vacuum-packed until use.

CANDIED PINE NUTS

Mix the water, sugar and the pine nuts together. Heat until it crisps up and carry on heating until candied. Roll out on silicone and separate. Sprinkle on the gold powder.

SEMI-CANDIED CHESTNUT

Pierce the chestnuts and place them for a few seconds in the microwave at 600W. Peel completely while still hot, then place them in a pressure cooker with the other ingredients for 5 minutes. Package and sous vide when ready to use.

VIOLET SAUCE

Infuse some of the gelatin with the violet oil and thicken with a small amount of chocolate. Sprinkle with pieces of the candied petals.

ASSEMBLY

Crumble the sponge on to the plate. At one end lay the chocolate cream with the chocolate crisp. At the other end of the sponge add a quenelle of ice cream and in the middle lay the pineapple flower. In the flour add the sautéed pineapple and decorate with a pansy. Decorate the plate with the pine nuts, chestnuts and violet sauce.

CHERRY & CHOCOLATE CAKE

ENTREMET, BY FRANCISCO JOSE SOMOZA ESTEVEZ MAKES 2 SERVES 8

INGREDIENTS

CHOCOLATE SPONGE CAKE

250g Almonds
225g Sugar
25g Honey
270g Eggs
50g Cocoa powder
50g Pastry flour
120g Melted butter

LYO CHERRY CRISP

150g Icing sugar
2g Apple pectin
50g Glucose
125g Butter
Lyo cherry

BLACK CHERRY JELLY

270g Cherry purée
25g Sugar
5g NH Pectin
1g Lemon juice

BLACK CHERRY
& CHOCOLATE CREAM

150g Cream
250g Black cherry purée
160g Egg yolks
100g Sugar
4 sheets Gelatine
140g Dark Guayaquil couverture
Griottines, as required

CARAMELISED CANE SUGAR
ESPUMA

250g Sugar
500g Whole milk
200g Egg yolks
16g Gelatine
750g Semi-whipped cream

CHOCOLATE/CHERRY GLAZE

125g Milk
125g Black cherry purée
50g Glucose
4 sheets Gelatine
600g Milk couverture

PROCESS

CHOCOLATE SPONGE CAKE

Place the almonds, sugar, honey and eggs in the food processor. Sieve the cocoa and flour and add to the whipped mixture. Lastly, add the butter and place in moulds. Cook at 200°C.

LYO CHERRY CRISP

Mix the sugar together with the pectin; add the glucose and softened butter. Scatter bits of Lyo cherry on top. Roll out on Silpat and cook at 200°C.

CARAMELISED CANE SUGAR
ESPUMA

Caramelize the sugar and de-glaze with the hot milk at 98°C. Make a crème Anglaise with the yolks, and caramel/milk mix. Add the softened gelatine. Lastly, fold in the semi-whipped cream.

BLACK CHERRY JELLY

Heat the purée to 40°C. Mix the sugar and pectin together. When it boils, add the juice and place in moulds.

BLACK CHERRY & CHOCOLATE
CREAM

Put the cream, purée, egg yolks and sugar in the Thermomix and heat to 85°C. Add the softened gelatine sheets. At intervals, pour over couverture – making an emulsion. Scatter with pieces of cherry.

CHOCOLATE/CHERRY GLAZE

Heat the milk, the purée and the glucose to 85°C. Add the softened gelatine. Pour over the chopped up couverture and whip without adding air. Serve at 30°C.

ASSEMBLY

In a 16cm cake tin make a layer of chocolate sponge, on top of this add the lyo cherry crisp and then a layer of the espuma. Freeze and then add a layer of cherry and chocolate cream, then another layer of espuma and then finally the black cherry jelly. Freeze and the remould in a 18cm cake tin. Coat with the remaining cream and freeze before coating with the chocolate/cherry glaze.

SWITZERLAND

WITH AN EXTRAORDINARY ABUNDANCE OF NATURAL BEAUTIES AND DESPITE IT'S VARIED GEOGRAPHICAL PATTERN AND THE DIFFERENCE IN LANGUAGE, RELIGION AND WAY OF LIFE AMONG ITS INHABITANTS, SWITZERLAND OFFERS AN ADMIRABLE EXAMPLE OF UNITY IN DIVERSITY.

Situated in the south of Central Europe, Switzerland mainly consists of mountains with no direct access to the sea. This was once considered a disadvantage to Switzerland, however its location at the very centre of the Alps thus making it the centre of Europe itself makes up for this. Switzerland is geographically divided between the Alps, the Central Plateau and the Jura. The Alps, providing unexpected treats for all sorts of walkers and without doubt one of the greatest mountain ranges, occupy the greater part of the territory however the Swiss population, made up of around 7.8 million people, is centered mostly around the Plateau, where the largest cities such as Zurich and Geneva can be found. Attracting those of all nationalities, Switzerland caters for all accommodation needs, providing everything from modest to luxurious, modern tourist facilities and a hospitable welcome, to suit every taste.

With a climate far from tropical and no colonies in cocoa-growing countries like South America or Africa it seems surprising that Switzerland has become one of the world's leading chocolate manufacturers. The Swiss are responsible for several breakthroughs in the technique of chocolate processing including the tempering process, the invention of the mixer which combined sugar and cocoa

powder and the invention of the conch which made for much smoother chocolate. Also masterminding combinations of hazelnut, milk and filled chocolate it is easy to see why the Swiss are masters of chocolate.

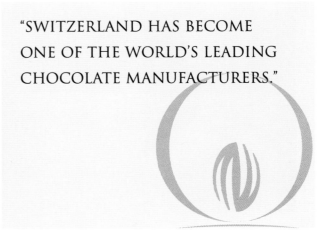

"SWITZERLAND HAS BECOME ONE OF THE WORLD'S LEADING CHOCOLATE MANUFACTURERS."

WINNER

CLAUDIA SCHMIDT

SWITZERLAND

CLAUDIA SCHMIDT

The 33 year-old confectioner and pastry chef Claudia Schmid has worked for Confiserie Sprüngli in production for more than a decade and is head of the ice cream department. In the Swiss Chocolate Masters Claudia was particularly noted for her artistic showpiece which is both striking and individual. Claudia is passionate about chocolate and looking forward to the competition final in Paris where she will represent Switzerland.

SECOND PLACE

PILAR RICCIARDI

Second place went to Argentinian born Pilar Riccardi who now lives in Geneva. Pilar is a confectioner at the Four Seasons Hotel des Bergues in Geneva but has a great deal of experience from around the world. Pilar competed well at the annual Swiss Bakery and Confectionery Fair (FBK) at Bern and was well organised at the competition.

THIRD PLACE

PASCAL INUAEN

Third place went to Pascal Inauen from Weissbad. The confectionary chef works at Hotel Hof Weissbad in Weissbad. Pascal is originally from Altstätten near the border of Austria, he has been a chef for many years and enjoyed taking part in the World Chocolate Masters preselection for Switzerland.

AZTEC GOLD

COATED PRALINE, BY CLAUDIA SCHMIDT MAKES 80

INGREDIENTS

PUMPKIN SEED GIANDUJA

75g Pumpkin seeds, roasted
75g Raw sugar
15g Pumpkin seed oil
15g Biscuit Raffinate
100g Milk couverture

VENEZUELA-GANACHE

250g Cream
60g Invert sugar (trimoline)
60g Butter
160g Couverture Venezuela
90g Couverture Onyx

Couverture Bourbon 'Swiss Top', to coat

PROCESS

PUMPKIN SEED GIANDUJA

Place the pumpkin seeds, roasted and the raw sugar in the Thermomix for 1 minute at Level 8. Add the pumpkin seed oil, biscuit raffinate and milk couverture, mix, warm up and spread out about 4mm thick.

VENEZUELA-GANACHE

Place the cream in the Thermomix for 3 minutes, Level 1-2, at 70°C. Add the invert sugar and butter and mix for 30 seconds. Add Couverture Venezuela drops and mix slowly on Level 1-2 for approximately 6 minutes. Cool down to 32°C. Pour out over the gianduja so that its about 12mm thick and leave to cool.

ASSEMBLY

Dip in Couverture Bourbon 'Swiss Top' and cool.

RELIEF

MOULDED PRALINE, BY CLAUDIA SCHMIDT MAKES 80

INGREDIENTS

RASPBERRY JELLY

100g Raspberry purée
60g Apricot purée
40g Glucose
70g Sugar
1g Pectin
40g Sugar
1g Citric acid

CALAMANSI CARAMEL

375g Sugar
112g Glucose
95g Water
75g Butter
280g Calamansi juice
190g Couverture, white

Coloured Cocoa Butter, to coat
Couverture Bourbon 'Swiss Top', to coat

PROCESS

RASPBERRY JELLY

Mix the raspberry purée, apricot purée, glucose and 70g sugar, bring to the boil. Mix the pectin and 40g sugar, add and heat to 95°C. Add the citric acid, mix, allow to cool down, mix again.

CALAMANSI CARAMEL

Bring the sugar, glucose and water to the boil, scrape the edges, boil until a caramel is formed. Add the butter and at approximately 40°C add the Calamansi juice slowly, heat to 110°C. Add the white couverture, mix, allow to cool.

ASSEMBLY

Coat moulds in cocoa butter and swiss top chocolate, fill with raspberry jelly and cool. Then fill with ganache and close.

THE TEOTIHUACAN HARVEST

PLATED DESSERT, BY CLAUDIA SCHMIDT SERVES 8

INGREDIENTS

TOMATO CHOCOLATE GANACHE

30g Raw sugar
70g Tomato juice
30g Tomato purée
25g Lemon juice
50g Cream
50g Couverture, white
15g Tomato flakes
8 ea. Hollow Body, dark

TOMATO CHOCOLATE COAT

80g Flour
4g Baking powder
30 Egg yolks
120g Water
50g Amaranth, popped
100g Breadcrumbs

SPONGE CAKE

80g Vanilla couverture
120g Egg whites
80g Egg yolks
80g Sugar
25g Flour

CHOCOLATE MOUSSE

250g Chocolate mousse (see Gift of the
God entrement recipe)
25g Peta Zeta

NOUGAT MOUSSE

80g Nougat Créme
140g Whipped cream
1g Gelatine

SPICE-CHOCOLATE

50g Couverture Onyx
2 Cinnamon
1 Black pepper
1g Paprika
1g Mace

CITRUS FRUIT COULIS

100g Cocktail d' Agrumes
80g Carma Brilliant Jelly
8 Physalis

CITRUS FRUIT AIR

80g Cocktail d'Agrumes
20g Lime Juice
3g Pure lecithin

PROCESS

TOMATO CHOCOLATE GANACHE

Place the raw sugar, tomato juice, tomato purée, lemon juice and cream in the Thermomix, Level 2, for 6 minutes at 70°C. Add the white couverture, mix briefly. Mix the tomato flakes into the cooled ganache, fill the hollow chocolate bodies and freeze.

TOMATO CHOCOLATE COAT

Mix the flour, baking powder, egg yolks and water together well. Cover the frozen chocolates with the mixture, coat with the popped amaranth and breadcrumbs and deep-fry at 180°C for 1 minute.

SPONGE CAKE

Mix all the ingredients together in a ISI-Whip with two No2 cartridges. Grease the moulds, fill to one-third. Microwave for 50 seconds.

CHOCOLATE MOUSSE

Mix all the ingredients together and fill in a mould – leave to chill until set.

NOUGAT MOUSSE

Mix all the ingredients together and fill in a mould – leave to chill until set.

SPICE-CHOCOLATE

Mix all the ingredients together, spread wafer-thin on a silpat and cut to size.

CITRUS FRUIT COULIS

Mix all the ingredients except the physalis together, heat slightly and arrange on the plate together with the cut physalis.

CITRUS FRUIT AIR

Mix all the ingredients together, allow to stand for a short while and skim off the foam, so that it can be arranged on the plate.

ASSEMBLY

Alternate the layers of chocolate and nougat mousse, separating with layers of spiced chocolate so that it forms a pyramid as pictured. Break the sponge up into pieces and place to one side of the pyramid. Use the coulis to decorate the plate and add the physalis, cover the physalis with the citrus air. Place the warm tomato-praline on the plate and serve immediately.

GIFT OF THE GOD

ENTREMET, BY CLAUDIA SCHMIDT MAKES 3 CAKES, EACH SERVES 10

INGREDIENTS

FLOUR-FREE BISCUIT

180g Egg yolk
80g Sugar
180g Couverture Onyx
180g Egg whites
80g Sugar

CHOCOLATE-PARFAIT DOUGH BASE

50g Whole egg
150g Sugar
100g Butter
50g Cocoa powder
200g Flour

CHOCOLATE MOUSSE

400g Milk
100g Egg yolks
95g Sugar
10g Gelatine
240g Couverture 'Grenada'
680g Whipped cream

MANGO STEW

50g Butter
70g Passionfruit juice
400g Mango cubes
30 Red peppercorns
3g Arrak liquor
6g Gelatine

MANGO-GINGER MOUSSE

120g Mango purée
40g Passionfruit juice
80g Invert sugar (trimoline)
10g Ginger
320g Couverture, white
8g Gelatine
800g Whipped cream

GLAZE

445g Cream
540g Water
665g Sugar
909g Glucose, solid
220g Cocoa powder
40g Gelatine

ASSEMBLY

Apricot jam, as needed

PROCESS

FLOUR-FREE BISCUIT

Mix together the 80g sugar and the egg yolks until fluffy and then add the Couverture Onyx. In a separate bowl whip together the egg whites and 80g sugar until the mix forms stiff peaks. Carefully fold this into the egg yolk mixture. Pour into three 16cm cake tins and bake at 160°C for 14 minutes.

CHOCOLATE-PARFAIT DOUGH BASE

Mix the eggs and sugar until fluffy, add the room temperature and continue to mix. Slowly sift in the flour and cocoa powder and briefly knead the mix to a dough. Roll out to 2.5mm, cut to size of a 19cm tin and bake for 12 minutes at 180°C.

CHOCOLATE MOUSSE

Place the milk, egg yolks and sugar in the Thermomix, Level 2, for 8 minutes at 90°C. Soak the gelatine and add. Add the Couverture 'Grenada' in drops, mix, cool down. Stir in the whipped cream thoroughly.

MANGO STEW

Heat the butter and passionfruit juice. Add the mango cubes and red peppercorns, boil slightly. Add the Arrak, boil down slightly and add the gelatine, stir and still slightly warm pour over the mousse.

MANGO-GINGER MOUSSE

Mix the Mango purée, passionfruit juice, invert sugar and ginger, heat slightly. Heat the white couverture add to the purée and mix. Soak the gelatine and when bloomed add. Mix in the whipped cream thoroughly.

GLAZE

Place the cream, water, sugar, glucose and cocoa powder in the Thermomix, Level 2, 100°C, for 12 minutes. Soak the gelatine and add. Allow the icing to crystallise overnight.

ASSEMBLY

Stick together the chocolate-parfait dough base and flour-free biscuit with apricot jam together. Then layer with the chocolate mousse, mango stew and then top with the mango-ginger mousse. Chill and when cool and firm cover with the glaze.

TAIWAN

ALTHOUGH TAIWAN IS A SMALL COUNTRY AND BARELY THE SIZE OF MANY AMERICAN STATES, TAIWAN IN FACT HAS MUCH TO OFFER AS A TOURIST DESTINATION WITH A VIBRANT CULTURE AND MANY WONDERFUL SIGHTS.

It also boasts a huge entertainment industry and is at the centre of Chinese pop culture. With scenery like the basalt cliffs of Penghu and the breath taking mountains of Wulai, Taiwan offers many magical sights and not to mention some of the world's best hot springs. Taiwanese cuisine, often based on influences from mid to southern provinces of Mainland China, also has a lot to offer and is acknowledged greatly among other Asians. A country with various cultural influences Taiwan boasts many exciting experiences and a fantastic slice of the Far East.

"A COUNTRY WITH VARIOUS CULTURAL INFLUENCES TAIWAN BOASTS MANY EXCITING EXPERIENCES AND A FANTASTIC SLICE OF THE FAR EAST."

WINNER

CHI HSIEN CHENG

TAIWAN

CHI HSIEN CHENG

Chi Hsien Cheng has always been interested in pastry and after watching his parents in the food industry he was passionate about improving his knowledge in the field. After his graduation from National Kaohslung University, Chi worked in luxury hotels, small business hotels and pastry boutiques for diversified experiences of work environments and management skills. Dedicated to improving his skills Chi Hsien has become silver winner of Chocolate Show Piece category in the Taiwan Gateaux Technique Contest and 3rd place in the Culinary Challenge in Singapore.

LITCHI CACAO

MOULDED PRALINE, BY CHI HSIEN CHENG MAKES 48

INGREDIENTS

RASPBERRY BRANDY JELLY

100g Raspberry purée
50g Water
100g Sugar
2g Yellow pectin
40g Raspberry brandy

ROSE LYCHEE AND
RASPBERRY GANACHE

69g Cream 36%
11g Trimoline
183g White chocolate
35g Rose lychee purée
13g Raspberry purée
14g Raspberry brandy
12g Butter

Raspberry powder, to sprinkle
50% cocoa bittersweet chocolate, to coat

PROCESS

RASPBERRY BRANDY JELLY

Boil the raspberry purée together with the water then add the sugar and pectin continuing to boil until the mixture reaches 105°C. Finally cool and then add the raspberry brandy.

ROSE LITCHI AND
RASPBERRY GANACHE

Boil the cream with the trimoline. Add in the white chocolate and mix well, then add the purées and mix again. Cool and then add the brandy and the butter and mix.

ASSEMBLY

Coat the moulds using 50% cocoa bittersweet chocolate and cool, then first pour the raspberry brandy jelly and cool. When cold top with the ganache, solidify and then coat with more 50% bittersweet chocolate to seal, sprinkle the base with raspberry powder before setting so attaches to the surface and eject the praline from the mould.

GIFT CHOCOLATE DESSERT

PLATED DESSERT, BY CHI HSIEN CHENG SERVES 6

INGREDIENTS

CHOCOLATE CAKE

168g Flour
2.5g Baking powder
19g Cocoa powder
122g Milk
55g Dark chocolate 64%
187g Whole egg
150g Butter
113g Almond paste
159g Sugar
22.5g Grand Marnier

CHOCOLATE CREAM

113g Cream 36%
13g Glucose
13g Trimoline
115g Dark chocolate 64%
38g Grand Marnier
205g Whipped cream 36%

BERRIES COMPOTE

15g Raspberry confit
50g Water
200g Sugar
238g Mixed frozen berries
30g Raspberry brandy

CHOCOLATE SHELL

Bittersweet chocolate with 50%, for the mould
Red cocoa butter, to coat

RASPBERRY CRUMBLE

150g Butter
100g Sugar
60g Almond ground
160g Flour
1g Salt
18g Raspberry powder

PROCESS

CHOCOLATE CAKE

Mix the flour, baking powder and cocoa powder. Boil milk and mix with chocolate then set aside to cool. Mix the butter, almond paste and sugar together, add the whole eggs and gradually add to the powdered ingredient. Finally add the chocolate milk and Grand Marnier and mix evenly. Pour into the desired mould and bake at 180°C for 18 minutes.

CHOCOLATE CREAM

Boil together the cream, glucose and Trimoline and mix into the chocolate. Add the Grand Marnier mix well and add the final 205g of cream.

BERRIES COMPOTE

Bring the raspberry confit, water and sugar to the boil. Add the frozen berries and begin to cool then add the raspberry brandy and mix well.

RASPBERRY CRUMBLE

Mix all ingredients together and chill. Cut into 1cm cubes and bake on a baking sheet for 10-15 minutes at 160°C until crispy.

ASSEMBLY

Use bittersweet chocolate with 50% to make round chocolate shell. In the bottom half of the shell fill with chocolate cake, then layer second half with chocolate cream and berry compote and sandwich the two halves together. Finally spray with red cocoa butter and decorate with raspberry crumble.

FEATHER

ENTREMET, BY CHI HSIEN CHENG MAKES 4 CAKES, EACH SERVES 8

INGREDIENTS

HAZELNUT & RASPBERRY DACQUOISE

125g Hazelnut, ground
50g Sugar
20g Raspberry powder
125g Egg white
110g Icing sugar
30g Butter

BANANA COMPOTE

400g Banana, sliced
50g Sugar
50g Brown sugar
1/2 Vanilla bean
30g Rum

CHOCOLATE CREAM

113g Whipped Cream 36%
13g Glucose
13g Trimoline
115g Dark chocolate 64%
205g Whipped cream 36%
38g Grand Marnier
1 sheet Gelatine, bloomed

PASSIONFRUIT CREAM

200g Whole egg
5 Egg yolks
160g Sugar
150g Passionfruit purée
15g Lemon juice
1 sheet Gelatine
300g Butter

CHOCOLATE MOUSSE

193g Egg yolk
54g Trimoline
268g Milk
4g Gelatine
310g Dark chocolate 64%
300g Whipped cream 36%

CHOCOLATE GLAZE

186g Water
293g Nappage Neutre
136g Sugar
1g Coffee essence
42g Cocoa powder
42g Chocolate 50%
20g Gelatin

CHOPPED ALMOND WITH RASPBERRY FLAVOUR

200g Almond, chopped
100g Icing sugar
100g Raspberry purée
Red colouring, as needed

PROCESS

HAZELNUT & RASPBERRY DACQUOISE

Mix together the hazelnut, sugar powder and raspberry powder together evenly. Combine the egg whites and icing sugar before adding to the mixture of hazelnut flour, sugar powder and raspberry powder. Finally at in the butter, cook at 180°C for 10 minutes.

BANANA COMPOTE

Caramelize the sugar, then add brown sugar, banana sliced and vanilla bean fry together. Last part is add rum to mix evenly with all ingredient.

CHOCOLATE CREAM

Boil the 113g whipped cream, trimoline syrup and glucose syrup. To the melted chocolate and 205g of cream add the gelatin and dissolve. Add Grand Marnier and mix well. Then add to the first whipped cream mix and fold in.

PASSIONFRUIT CREAM

Mix the whole egg, egg yolk and sugar well. Boil the passionfruit purée and lemon juice, add the egg mixture and blend well, then sieve and return to the boil. Add the soaked Gelatin and mix evenly, gradually cool to 60°C and add the melted butter and mix well.

CHOCOLATE MOUSSE

Boil together egg yolk, milk and trimoline. Soak the gelatin and add to the chocolate mix, add the whipped cream and mix well.

CHOCOLATE GLAZE

Mix together the water, nappage neutre, sugar, coffee – mix and boil together. Add the cocoa powder, the chocolate and soaked gelatin and then boil. Sieve and then cool to 38°C.

CHOPPED ALMOND WITH RASPBERRY FLAVOUR

Mix all the ingredients and place on a silpat mat, then put into the oven with 130°C and bake until crispy.

ASSEMBLY

Pour the dacquoisie into the bottom of a 16cm cake tin, then add the banana compote, then a layer of chocolate cream and freeze. Then add a layer of passionfruit cream and freeze. Demould and place in a 18cm cake tin. Coat with chocolate mousse, freeze and then glaze. Decorate with raspberry almonds.

UNITED KINGDOM

DOMINATED BY A RUGGED SHORELINE AND ANCIENT HISTORY, THE UNITED KINGDOM IS MADE UP OF FOUR COUNTRIES: ENGLAND, WALES, SCOTLAND AND NORTHERN IRELAND.

England itself is comprised of some beautiful counties all of which offer a slight difference in culture and lifestyle. Home to the most visited international city in the world, London, this unique capital city is known for its world-famous attractions – from Big Ben to Buckingham Palace, there are hundreds of sights on offer which top every tourist's must-see list. There is also the country of Wales which personifies natural beauty with its mountain peaks, brooding forests and national parks, beautiful beaches and broad rivers and lakes.

Scotland on the other hand is a constant surprise to its visitors who travel from all over the world. The remote wilderness scenery of the Highlands and Islands contrasts with the peaceful Trossachs and the rich farmlands of the Borders, while the great lowland cities of Glasgow and the nation's capital, Edinburgh, remain its commercial and cultural heartbeat. The UK chocolate industry is worth £3.6 billion and the UK currently has the seventh highest consumption of chocolate in the world with the average Brit eating 17.49lbs of chocolate per year.

"THE UK CHOCOLATE INDUSTRY IS WORTH £3.6 BILLION AND THE UK CURRENTLY HAS THE SEVENTH HIGHEST CONSUMPTION OF CHOCOLATE IN THE WORLD."

WINNER

JOHN COSTELLO

UNITED KINGDOM

JOHN COSTELLO

John has gained experience at many established companies including family run artisan company, Slatterys. Having taken various courses in chocolate showpieces and sugarcraft John has also learnt his skills competing in competitions all over the world. John is a previous contestant of the UK Chocolate Masters and has recently take part in the World Pastry Team Championships in Phoenix. In the past he has won titles such as the Renshaw cup and Pierre Scacco Award. Currently, John is employed by Park Cakes.

SECOND PLACE

RUTH HINKS

Ruth currently works for chocolatier Cocoa Black in Peebles Scotland. Originally from South Africa she has worked in cities such Melbourne and Cape Town among others. Used to competitions Ruth has taken part in the Culinary Olympics in both 2000 and 2004 in Germany. An experienced chocolatier Ruth has worked with chocolate for over 25 years and enjoys testing her creativity and technical skills in a competition environment.

THIRD PLACE

GRAHAM HORNIGOLD

After receiving a degree in international culinary arts management 2007 at Thames Valley University, Graham has gone on to win the UK Tea Guild Best Afternoon Tea twice. Now working for the Manderin Oriental hotel in Hyde Park as Chef Patissier, Graham is always looking for new ways to pass on his knowledge to his team.

TROPICAL TWIST

COATED PRALINE, BY JOHN COSTELLO MAKES 80

INGREDIENTS

PASSIONFRUIT PATE D'FRUIT

100g Passionfruit purée
100g Apple juice
40g Sugar
12g Pectin
190g Sugar

STAR ANISE GANACHE

150g Alto El Sol
180g Cream
23g Glucose
23g Butter
4g Star anise

Alto el sol dark chocolate, to coat

PROCESS

PASSIONFRUIT PATE D'FRUIT

Bring the apple juice and purée to the boil. Mix together the 40g sugar and pectin and add to the apple juice mix. Slowly add the 190g sugar and cook to 107°C. Cool slightly and pour into a 8mm frame, when the density is 74B-Brix remove from the frame and replace with a 16mm frame.

STAR ANISE GANACHE

Place all ingredients into Mycook/ Thermomix and heat to 40°C on slow speed. Pour into the frame on top of the jelly layer. Pour the ganache on top and allow to set.

ASSEMBLY

When the ganache has set remove from the frame and coat the jelly side with a thin layer of dark chocolate. Cut with guitar cutter. Dip in dark chocolate and decorate.

AZTEC PUNCH

MOULDED PRALINE, BY JOHN COSTELLO MAKES 84

INGREDIENTS

TEQUILA GANACHE

200g Lime caramel
200g Dark Mexican
10g Butter
18g Tequila

SALTED LIME CARAMEL

5g Sea salt
375g Sugar
75g Lime purée
150g Cream 35%

Green cocoa butter, to spray
Yellow cocoa butter, to spray
Mexican milk chocolate, for the moulds

PROCESS

TEQUILA GANACHE

Pour warm caramel over the chocolate, emulsify then add the butter and Tequila.

SALTED LIME CARAMEL

Make a dry caramel with the salt and sugar then deglaze with warm purée and the cream over a medium heat until caramelized.

ASSEMBLY

Spray the mould with green cocoa butter. Spray the mould with yellow cocoa butter. Coat with tempered Mexican milk chocolate. Pipe in the caramel. Pipe in the ganache. Pour chocolate on the back of the mould and seal with a transfer sheet.

MAYAN GOLD

PLATED DESSERT, BY JOHN COSTELLO SERVES 6

INGREDIENTS

YELLOW CURVES

100g White chocolate
10g Yellow cocoa butter

APRICOT COMPOTE

375g Apricots, diced
60g Sugar
22g Butter
2g Pectin
12g Sugar
2g Gelatine
12g Water

PRALINE CRUNCH

800g Praline Feuilletine
200g Bres

SPICED SPONGE

95g Flour
45g Ground hazelnuts
45g Icing sugar
10g Cinnamon
2g Nutmeg
4g Star anise
95g Honey
110g Egg yolks
65g Egg
10g Orange zest
140g Tanzania chocolate
140g Butter
240g Egg whites
55g Brown sugar

APRICOT CHOCOLATE MOUSSE

120g Apricot purée
40g Cream
40g Mexican dark chocolate
280g Mexican milk chocolate
100g Cream
100g Vanilla infused cocoa butter
200g Dark chocolate
30g Red cocoa butter

CHOCOLATE APRICOT AND PRALINE SORBET

300g Gia
250g Apricot purée
250g Water
60g Glucose

CRUNCH LAYER

100g Cocoa Nibs
100g Bres

APRICOT SAUCE

250g Apricot purée
30g Water
50g Sugar
0.5g Pectin
10g Sugar

ASSEMBLY

Yellow cocoa butter, to spray
Red cocoa butter, to spray

PROCESS

YELLOW CURVES

Temper and mix together until smooth then pipe lines onto a plastic sheet and curve, place a plaque on the back and leave to crystallize before using.

APRICOT COMPOTE

Boil together the diced apricots, 60g sugar and butter. Mix together the pectin and the 12g of sugar then mix into the apricot mixture. Soak the gelatin and water together then add to the apricot mixture and leave to cool.

PRALINE CRUNCH

Warm both the ingredients together then spread between plastic sheets refrigerate and cut into 10cm x 1.5cm pieces.

SPICED SPONGE

Sieve together the flour, ground hazelnut, icing sugar, cinnamon, nutmeg and star anise. Mix the honey, egg yolks and egg together and add to the flour mix. Add the orange zest and mix into the sponge mix. Melt the chocolate and butter together, then add to the mixture and mix together. Whisk the egg white and brown sugar together and fold into the mix. Pour into a tin and bake at 160°C for 30 minutes. When cool cut to 3 x 10cm rectangles.

APRICOT CHOCOLATE MOUSSE

Mix the purée, 40g of cream and both chocolates in a Thermomix at 40°C. Whip the 100g of cream until around three-quarters whipped and fold into the chocolate mix. Pipe into mould then freeze, when frozen spray with milk chocolate spray, made from heating the remaining ingredients to 40°C.

CHOCOLATE, APRICOT AND PRALINE SORBET

Place into a Thermomix and heat to 100°C then pour into a Pacojet flask and freeze. Once frozen churn and pipe into a mould.

CRUNCH LAYER

Grind the ingredients to a powder.

APRICOT SAUCE

Bring the apricot purée, water and sugar to the boil. Mix the pectin and the 10g sugar together and then add to the apricot mixture and cook for 3 minutes then cool.

CHOCOLATE PLAQUE

Spread chocolate thin onto plastic then mark into 100mm x 15mm plaques, place plastic on top and put a tray on top to avoid curving.

ASSEMBLY

Brush the sauce onto a plate. Place the spiced sponge onto the edge of sauce. Place praline crunch onto spiced sponge then add a layer of compote on top of that. Place the plaque and curves onto the compote layer and on top of that place the apricot mousse. At the opposite end of the plate place small amount of crunch layer. Make a quenelle and then spray with yellow cocoa butter, then red cocoa butter, place onto crunch layer and serve.

SABROSO

ENTREMET, BY JOHN COSTELLO MAKES 3 CAKES, EACH SERVES 8

INGREDIENTS

CHOCOLATE BROWNIE

80g Tanzania cocoa powder
140g Flour
30g Water
580g Sugar
2 Madagascan vanilla pods
350g Eggs
370g Tanzania chocolate
426g Butter

CHOCOLATE GLAZE

94g Water
563g Cream
825g Sugar
225g Tanzania cocoa powder
22g Gelatin
113g Water

RASPBERRY COMPOTE

375g Raspberries
60g Sugar
22g Butter
3g Pectin
12g Sugar
4g Gelatin
24g Water

PRALINE CRUNCH

800g Praline Feuilletine
200g Bres

CHOCOLATE SABLE

240g Salted butter
240g Icing sugar
120g Egg yolks
270g Flour
14g Baking Powder
70g Tanzania cocoa powder
Mycryo, as needed

VANILLA CREAM

402g Milk
1 Vanilla pod
78g Egg yolks
102g Sugar
30g Mycryo
9g Gelatin
48g Raspberry liquor
300g Cream

RASPBERRY JELLY

420g Raspberry purée
20g Lemon purée
116g Sugar
24g Starch
8g Gelatin
48g Water

MOUSSE

430g Caramel
60g Cream
450g Madirofolo Chocolate
650g Cream

PROCESS

CHOCOLATE BROWNIE

Sieve together the Tanzania cocoa powder and flour into a mixing bowl. Combine the water and sugar then add to the dry ingredients. Mix the vanilla pods with the eggs and then add to the mixture. Melt together the Tanzania chocolate and butter and add to the mix. Bake in the oven at 160°C for 25-30 minutes.

CHOCOLATE GLAZE

Heat together the water, cream and sugar. over a medium heat the slowly add the Tanzania cocoa powder. Soak the gelatin in the water, add then strain the mixture.

RASPBERRY COMPOTE

Boil together the raspberries, 60g sugar and butter. Mix together the pectin and 12g sugar, then add to the raspberry mixture. Soak the gelatine in the water and add to the raspberry mixture.

PRALINE CRUNCH

Warm the ingredients together, then spread between plastic sheets, and cut to shape.

CHOCOLATE SABLE

Mix together the butter and icing sugar. Slowly add the egg yolks. Sieve together the flour, baking powder and Tanzania cocoa powder and add to the rest of the mixture and chill. Then when cool roll out to 3mm thick. Bake at 160°C for 10-12 minutes. Sprinkle with Mycryo on removal from the oven and cut.

VANILLA CREAM

Cook together the milk, vanilla pod, egg yolks and sugar. Add the Mycryo. Soak the gelatin in the raspberry liquor; add to the mixture and leave to cook. Whip the cream and fold through the mixture.

RASPBERRY JELLY

Heat the purées together. Mix together the sugar and starch and add slowly to the purées. Soak the gelatine in the water and add to the mixture.

MOUSSE

Melt together the caramel, cream and Madirofolo chocolate and cool. Whip the cream and fold into the mixture.

ASSEMBLY

To make the centre, pour vanilla into 6 x 6mm thick moulds and freeze. Place 3 x 3mm mould on top of three of the first moulds. Pour raspberry jelly into the three and freeze. Remove from the moulds and place the vanilla slices on top of the raspberry and vanilla. Cut the brownie into 6mm thick slices. Stack the three vanilla and raspberry stacks together and place a slice of brownie between each layer.

To make the chocolate pastry, place the sable into the frame. Place on crunch layer. Place raspberry compote. Pipe in raspberry mousse 10mm in height. Place in frozen insert. Pipe mousse to top of frame and freeze. Remove from freezer and glaze. Garnish with flower and plaques.

USA

AT 3.79 MILLION SQUARE MILES AND WITH OVER 308 MILLION PEOPLE, THE UNITED STATES OF AMERICA IS A FEDERAL CONSTITUTIONAL REPUBLIC COMPRISING FIFTY STATES AND A FEDERAL DISTRICT.

The country is situated mostly in central North America, where its forty-eight contiguous states and Washington, D.C., the capital district, lie between the Pacific and Atlantic Oceans, bordered by Canada to the north and Mexico to the south. America is the birthplace of LA, Las Vegas, Chicago, Miami, Boston and New York City – an array of dazzling states, each has something different to offer with a million different notions of culture, cuisine and entertainment. Look more closely and you will find many natural and cultural wonders, from the outstanding waterfront of San Francisco to the eclectic music scene of Austin. A country of road trips and great open skies, The United States of America provides every scene imaginable.

Chocolate is as popular in the United States as the rest of the world and is seen as one of the biggest chocolate distributors in the world. Beginning in 1765, during the American Revolutionary War, the first chocolate factory was established in America. Chocolate is a multi-million dollar business in the United States and it imports more chocolate per capita than anywhere else in the world. With chocolate used in desserts, cereals, sauces, drinks and paired with flavours such as peanut butter and marshmallow, it seems there is no stopping the world's favourite product.

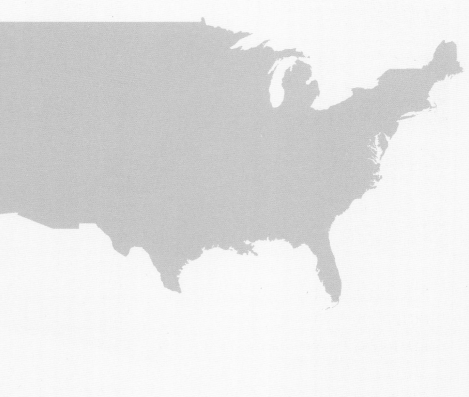

"CHOCOLATE IS A MULTI-MILLION DOLLAR BUSINESS IN THE UNITED STATES AND IT IMPORTS MORE CHOCOLATE PER CAPITA THAN ANYWHERE ELSE IN THE WORLD."

WINNER

SYLVAIN BORTOLINI

USA

SYLVAIN BORTOLINI

Sylvain Bortolini began his training at the Association Ouvriéres Des Compagnons Du Tour De France in Bordeaux in France. Prior to joining the Bellagio resort in Las Vegas, Nevada, Sylvain has worked as a pastry chef at the Fontainebleau Miami Beach resort in Florida and the InterContinental Presidente hotel in Mexico City. In 2007, he won the Mexican Pastry Championship for his sugar work and chocolate sculpture. Sylvain has also served as pastry chef for two star Michelin-rated restaurants and gourmet chocolate shops in France.

PAPANTLA

COATED PRALINE, BY SYLVAIN BORTOLINI MAKES 45

INGREDIENTS

Praline Amande 65% Fruits

PAPANTLA VANILLA GANACHE

226g Heavy cream 34%
35g Butter
5g Vanilla bean
30g Sorbitol
125g Lactee Superieur
232g Alto del Sol
6.3g Mycryo
52 Dextrose

ALMOND PRALINE

650g Whole almonds
350g Granulated Sugar
100g Water
2 Vanilla beans

Fleur de Cao, to coat

PROCESS

ALMOND PRALINE

Roast the almonds in the oven at 160°C for 5 minutes. Heat the sugar and the water to 130°C. Pour the warm almonds into it with the vanilla beans. Caramelise the almonds until they turn brown then place on a silpat to cool. When the almonds are at room temperature process them with a Robot Coupe or food processor.

PAPANTLA VANILLA GANACHE

Warm up the cream with the butter, the vanilla bean, the sorbitol and the dextrose powder. Leave this mix to infuse for 10 minutes then pour the hot cream into the robot coupe while processing. Add the Mycryo and mix.

ASSEMBLY

Layer the ganache on top of the praline and coat with Fleur de Cao. Decorate with a caramelised almond.

CARAMEL BLACKCURRANT

MOULDED PRALINE, BY SYLVAIN BORTOLINI MAKES 45

INGREDIENTS

BLACKBERRY GANACHE

110g Blackcurrant purée
30g Cream 35%
25g Butter
25g Sorbitol
60g Granulated Sugar
20g Cassis Liqueur
226g Lactée Supérieure
22g Fleur de Cao
12g Mycryo

Lactee Superieur, to coat

PROCESS

BLACKBERRY GANACHE

Warm up the blackcurrant purée with the cream, butter and sorbitol. Make a dry caramel with the sugar over a low heat. Pour the blackcurrant mixture into the caramel and lightly boil. Put the chocolate couvertures into a Robot Coupe and then pour the caramel cassis cream mix into it. Add the Mycryo and the cassis alcohol and process together until smooth.

ASSEMBLY

Coat a mould with Lactee Superieur and pour the caramel blackcurrant ganache into the mould and close.

FLEUR DE CAO

PLATED DESSERT, BY SYLVAIN BORTOLINI SERVES 10

INGREDIENTS

FLEUR DE CAO TRUFFLE (INSIDE THE BEIGNET)

250g Heavy Cream
20g Lactée Supérieure
40g Butter
150g Fleur de Cao

HOMEMADE PRALINE

25g Mycryo
25g Couverture Lactée Supérieure
250g Praline paste
50g Feuilletine

FLEUR DE CAO CHOCOLATE MOUSSE

250g Whole Milk
375g Fleur de Cao
7g Gelatine Sheet
500g Heavy Cream 35%

PEAR COMPTEE

750g Fresh pear, cut into small cubes
150g Granulated Sugar
3g Vanilla bean from Papantla
50g Lemon juice
100g Pear purée
2g Agar Agar
40g Williamine

CHOCOLATE SORBET

525g Water
300g Granulated Sugar
35g Trimoline
2g Cremodan
250g Fleur de Cao
100g Whole Milk

CHOCOLATE BEIGNET DOUGH

275g AP Flour
37g Cacao powder
182g Whole Milk
37g Melted Butter
1g Salt
112g Granulated Sugar
1.5 g Baking Powder
62g Eggs
120g Water

ISOMALT DECORATION

500g Isomalt
50g Water

PROCESS

FLEUR DE CAO TRUFFLE

Boil the heavy cream and pour into the chocolate. Cool the mixture and when the ganache is under 40°C add the buerre pommade. Pour the ganache mix into the truffle shell. Once the ganache has crystallised close the truffle.

HOMEMADE PRALINE

Melt the Mycryo with the milk couverture. Mix it with the praline paste and the feuilletine. Bring it down to 21°C. Pour into the small frame.

FLEUR DE CAO CHOCOLATE MOUSSE

Boil the milk and pour into the fleur de cao chocolate. Add the gelatine sheet. Whip the heavy cream and add it to the ganache.

PEAR COMPTEE

Cut the fresh pears into small pieces. Make a caramel with the sugar and cook the pears in it with the vanilla bean for 10 minutes. At the end add the lemon juice, the purée and the agar agar. Finally add the williamine.

CHOCOLATE SORBET

Make a syrup with the water, sugar, trimoline and the cremodan and boil for 2 minutes. Let the mix cool down to 45°C, add the chocolate and blend it in. Once cold add the milk and process with an ice cream machine according to the manufacturer's instructions.

CHOCOLATE BEIGNET DOUGH

Put the flour, cacao powder, salt, sugar, baking powder all together in the kitchen aid. Slowly incorporate the eggs, milk and the water. At the end add the melted butter until it has become a dough. Make to shape around the truffle and dip fry for a few minutes until crispy.

ISOMALT DECORATION

Add the isomalt to the water and cook the mix until it reaches 162°C. When still hot pull it round a rolling pin to give a shape.

ASSEMBLY

Pipe a rectangle of praline and then on top pipe a layer of Fleur de Cao chocolate mousse, finally layer with pear comptee. Place on top of the a quenelle of chocolate sorbet and the chocolate Beignet. Decorate with the isomalt decoration.

ALTO DEL SOL

ENTREMET, BY SYLVAIN BORTOLINI SERVES 16

INGREDIENTS

LEMON CREAM

150g Fresh lemon juice
150g Whole eggs
135g Granulated sugar
2.3g Gelatine, melted
150g Butter
37.5 g Mycryo

GLANDUJA CREMEUX

93g Glanduja Plaisir Lenôtre
30g Hazelnut paste
93g Heavy cream 34%
2.6g Gelatine, melted
187g Heavy cream 34%, whipped

HAZELNUT DACQUOISE

185g Egg whites
135g Granulated Sugar
115g Hazelnut powder
70g Sugar powder
40g Flour T-45

FLOURLESS CHOCOLATE BISCUIT

16g Cacao paste
120g Alto del Sol
75g Butter
76g Egg yolks
33g Granulated sugar
144g Egg whites

ALTO DEL SOL CHOCOLATE MOUSSE

250g Whole milk
375g Alto del Sol
7g Gelatine sheet
500g Heavy cream 35%

DARK GLAZE

360g Granulated sugar
290g Water
240g Heavy cream 34%
120g Cocoa powder
50g Glucose
17g Gelatine, melted

PROCESS

LEMON CREAM

Boil the fresh lemon juice. Blanchir (whip) the whole eggs with the sugar and pour the lemon juice into it. Put the mix back into the pan and boil for 2 minutes. Let the cream cool down to 60°C and add the gelatine. Add the butter and Mycryo to the mixture and stir.

GLANDUJA CRÉMEUX

Make a ganache with the Gianduja, the hazelnut paste and the 93g heavy cream. Add the melted gelatine and finally add the 187g whipped cream and mix together.

HAZELNUT DACQUOISE

Sift the powders and flour three times. Whip the egg whites with the sugar. Slowly mix the powders and flour into the meringue. Cut into shapes on a baking tray and bake at 160°C for 5 minutes.

FLOURLESS CHOCOLATE BISCUIT

Melt the cacao paste with the alto del sol and the butter. Whip the egg yolks and half of the of the sugar and mix it with the chocolate. Whip the egg whites with the second half of the sugar and slowly mix all together. Cut into shapes on a baking tray. Bake at 175°C until risen.

ALTO DEL SOL CHOCOLATE MOUSSE

Boil the milk and pour into the Alto del Sol. Add the gelatine sheet. Whip the heavy cream and add it to the ganache.

DARK GLAZE

Cook all the ingredients together until the mix reaches 99°C. Cool and add the gelatine at under 60°C. Glaze the cake at 45°C.

ASSEMBLY

In a 18cm cake tin layer the hazlenut croquant, then follow with a layer of lemon cream, a thick layer of dacquoise, another layer of lemon cream then the hazelnut cremeux and a thick layer of chocolate mousse before coating with glaze. Decorate as desired.

dare to break the mould

WANT TO HAVE YOUR OWN COPY OF THE MAGAZINE ALL THE TOP CHEFS ARE READING?

Moderated by an editorial board consisting of a team of well-known and respected chefs, *Chef Magazine* provides original, accurate and up to date information that is guaranteed to be informative and authoritative. With in-depth interviews with some of the most highly regarded chefs in the industry, discussions on industry topics, reviews of kitchen equipment and a lot more, *Chef Magazine* is an essential tool in any professional kitchen.

The first choice for professional chefs

⤵ IN NEED OF HELPFUL HINTS FROM THE BEST IN THE BUSINESS?

⤵ EAGER TO FIND OUT THE LATEST ON FOOD TRENDS?

⤵ HUNGRY FOR THE INSIDE GOSSIP ON THE HOTTEST INGREDIENTS?

⤵ FASCINATED BY THE SKILLS OF TODAY'S TOP CHEFS?

6 ISSUES FOR ONLY £25. SUBSCRIBE NOW TO CHEF MAGAZINE AND AUTOMATICALLY BECOME A MEMBER OF THE CHEF PRIVILEGE CLUB

visit **www.chefmagazine.co.uk**

PRIVILEGE CHEF CLUB

UK £25.00 *including postage* EU £41.00 *including postage* REST OF WORLD £55.00 *including postage*

RETURN TO: CHEF MAGAZINE LTD, NETWORK HOUSE, 28 BALLMOOR, CELTIC COURT, BUCKINGHAM, MK18 1RQ

TEL: 01280 829300 FAX: 01280 829326 EMAIL: INFO@CHEFMAGAZINE.CO.UK

OR ALTERNATIVELY SUBSCRIBE ON OUR WEBSITE AT: WWW.CHEFMAGAZINE.CO.UK/SUBSCRIBE

JOIN OUR CLUB

CO PRIVILEGE CHEF CLUB

DEDICATED TO OFFERING THE VERY BEST OFFERS TO CHEFS AND OTHER PROFESSIONALS IN THE INDUSTRY THE CHEF MAGAZINE CHEF PRIVILEGE CLUB IS GIVING SOMETHING BACK TO CHEFS.

Whether its networking with fellow chef club members, tasting wine in the vineyards of Rioja, truffle hunting with a chef legend or a factory visit to a supplier of your favourite brand — all these experiences and more can be found within the Chef Privilege Club.

As well as this members of the club will receive exclusive, previously unavailable discounts on products from pans to cookbooks, restaurants to wine.

Subscribe to Chef Magazine and you also become a member of our exclusive Chef Privilege Club.

ALREADY A SUBSCRIBER?

Once registered as a subscriber, log in to www.chefmagazine.co.uk to gain access to exciting events, exclusive offers and the chance to experience one-off gastronomic explorations.

RECIPE INDEX

NOTES

NOTES